THE
VANISHING
MINISTRY

THE VANISHING MINISTRY

Woodrow Kroll

KREGEL PUBLICATIONS
Grand Rapids, Michigan 49501

The Vanishing Ministry by Woodrow Kroll. © 1991 by Woodrow Kroll and published in 1991 by Kregel Publications, a division of Kregel, Inc. P. O. Box 2607, Grand Rapids, MI 49501. All rights reserved.

Cover & Book Design: Al Hartman

Library of Congress Cataloging-in-Publication Data

Kroll, Woodrow M. (Woodrow Michael), 1944-
  The vanishing ministry / Woodrow Kroll.
     p. cm.
  1. Clergy—Office. 2. Pastoral Theology. I. Title.
BV660.2K77   1991   262'.1—dc20   91-11752
                                      CIP
ISBN   0-8254-3057-7 (pbk.)

1 2 3 4 5 Printing/Year 95 94 93 92 91

Printed in the United States of America

This book
is dedicated to
BRYAN KROLL
1967 — 1987

Contents

Preface 9

Part One: The Mess of Reality   13

How are we really doing?

1. Stated Goals 15
2. Smashed Goals 17
3. America as a Sending Nation 25
4. America as a Mission Field 29

Part Two: The Devilish Diversion   37

How did we get where we are?

5. Secular Self-Interest 39
6. Upward Mobility Parents 43
7. WAGAPS Elementary Teachers 49
8. The Abandoned Ministry Mission 53
9. The Blitzkrieg Call 59
10. Eli Syndrome Pastors 65

Part Three: The Company of the Committed   73

What attitudes are needed for ministry?

11. The Attitude of Commitment 75
12. The Attitude of Compassion 79

13. The Attitude of Pliability 85
14. The Attitude of Expendability 91
15. The Attitude of Ownership 95

Part Four: The Road Back   105

Where do we go from here?

16. Heritage Parents 107
17. Barnabas Pastors 111
18. Ministry Education 117
19. Aggressive Churches 121
20. Sensitive Seasons 127
21. Bridge Burning 135
22. Spiritual Vision 141

    Epilogue 147

    Notes 153

    Appendix 157

Preface

The Vanishing Ministry. It happened without fanfare — in fact, without notice. While the church slept, the great diverter worked diligently.

He got us inordinately interested in ourselves. He distorted our goals for our children. He got pastors too busy with today's problems to be aware of tomorrow's needs. He got our Christian colleges to broaden their scope and consequently dilute their emphasis. He attacked on every front simultaneously. It matters little toward whom the finger of blame points. It was no one's fault; it was everyone's fault. We were all taken in by the devil's devices.

The result wasn't felt immediately. In many areas, it wasn't recognized at all. Usually we do not even know we have a problem until it's too late for a solution. But, we have a problem!

The ministry work force is vanishing before our eyes. Mission stations close every day, and it never makes the newspaper. Churches close and some town residents barely take notice. Fewer young people hear the call to ministry and little is done. The great diverter is good at his job.

This book assesses the state of lifetime ministry at the threshold of the 21st century. By lifetime ministry I mean any ministry of the Word that demands a person subject his or her goals and plans to the eternal

9

purpose of God and submit himself or herself to God's call to service as a life and livelihood. It may elsewhere be called career ministry or full-time ministry, but it is a ministry of the Word that lasts a lifetime.

The Vanishing Ministry is comprised of four divisions. Part One considers the state of lifetime ministry today and soberly asks the question, "How are we really doing?" Part Two assesses the conditions which have contributed to the present decline in lifetime ministry and have aided the vanishing ministry. Part Three addresses primary attitudes which must be present in the thinking of men and women if they are to be sensitive to the call of God on their lives. And Part Four describes the road back, what must be done if the vanishing ministry is to stop vanishing.

The Vanishing Ministry is not just the title of this book; it is a disastrous reality. It is a problem that rivals in impact the lethargy and excess out of which came the Protestant Reformation. Perhaps it is a problem the solution for which will rival the Reformation in importance.

WOODROW KROLL

Lincoln, Nebraska
January 1, 1991

Part One

The Mess of Reality

How are we really doing?

The Mess of Reality

How are we really doing?

When the Lord Jesus said, "Upon this rock I will build my church; and the gates of hell shall not prevail against it" (Matt. 16:18), we embarked on a magnificent obsession. Win the lost at any cost.

His command, "Go ye into all the world, and preach the gospel to every creature" (Mark 16:15) was met with unbridled enthusiasm. Generation after generation has seen bright, dedicated young people give up their homes, their loved ones, their careers and more to carry the message of Christ's redeeming love to the ends of the earth.

The story is the same in this century. In spite of the danger, the deprivation, the personal sacrifice, there are well over 80,000 Protestant missionaries and 138,000 Roman Catholic missionaries in the world today.[1] Scores of mission agencies have been raised up to coordinate these soldiers of the cross as they depart for the four corners of the world. Currently there are 395 agencies engaged in sending career personnel overseas, and that's an increase from 371 in 1985.[2]

Churches, too, have responded as the sending agencies of the missionary. In 1988 Christians contributed $1,727,100,000 of their incomes to finance the overseas missionary enterprise.[3]

Are these efforts paying off? Absolutely. Consider this. A total of

1,684,535,500 persons claimed allegiance to the Christian religion in 1988 (33% of the world's 5.1 billion people), somewhat less than twice the number of adherents to Islam, the second largest religion with nearly a billion followers. David Bryant says that every day the number of Christians grows by an estimated 60,000 new believers in Jesus Christ as Saviour. This results in 1600 new churches opening their doors every Sunday for the first time.[4] That's exciting!

– 1 –

Stated Goals

With this as our history, and with an event approaching that has only occurred once since Jesus walked the sands of Judaea (the dawn of a new millennium — A.D. 2000), mission agencies and missiologists of North America and the world set their sights on the future. At the forefront of the A.D. 2000 movement is the distinguished missionary visionary Ralph Winter who comments, "Never before have the stakes been so high, or the opportunity so great. Never before has it been so impellingly possible for us to give our utmost for his highest."[5]

None of us would disagree. These are exciting days in which to live. We all recognize that if this generation is to be reached for Christ, we must reach it. The last generation had its chance; the next generation will have its chance. But this is our generation, and we have only one chance to reach it. Whether we succeed or fail cannot be blamed on the last generation and cannot be projected to the next. We are the only army on the battlefield right now.

Buoyed by advances in technology, many mission agencies focused on the end of the 20th century and established significant goals for their constituents. The momentum is there and is building for the A.D. 2000 movement. Presently there are nearly 100 "mega-plans" to reach the world for Christ by the year 2000. Decades ago Southern Baptists began talking about taking the message of the gospel to every person on earth by the year 2000. United Methodists challenged their people to double church membership in the USA by the century's end. More than three decades ago premier evangelist Billy Graham called for the world to be evangelized completely in one decade.

In the 1973 edition of Mission Handbook, respected missiologist J. Herbert Kane wrote that "Campus Crusade for Christ is greatly expanding its overseas work and hopes to complete the evangelization of the world in the next decade."[6] That date again was 1973.

Of the setting of goals there is no end. We need them; we live by them. Without goals the missionary enterprise would be static. And as the 21st century dawns the setting of goals to reach the world increases. In spite of the flurry of activity, a note of realism needs to be sounded. Barrett and Reapsome have documented that nearly half of the 788 world-capturing visions since the days of the apostles have sputtered on the launching pad.[7] It will take more than plans, programs and projections to win the world for Christ. It will take a basic restructuring of finances, attitudes and approaches.

Although I am pleased and genuinely rejoice at what has been done and what is being planned in missions, I fear many of today's plans may reflect only the cleanliness of theory. But as so aptly has been said, "The cleanliness of theory is no match for the mess of reality." What is reality?

Let's examine how we're really doing!

– 2 –

Smashed Goals

As much as we'd like to think that the missionary enterprise is going well, and in some areas of the world it is, overall there is much more to be done than has been done. Yes, there are victories, tremendous victories. There are areas of the world where the gospel is changing the face of the earth.

For example, it is believed that there were 4,000,000 African Christians in 1900 (3 percent of the population). By the year 2000 that number is estimated to be 351,000,000 African Christians (46 percent of the population). The number today is 212,000,000. Christianity in the Two-Thirds World has spread like wildfire. According to David Barrett, in 1989 there were 75,000,000 East Asian Christians compared to 16,000,000 in 1980, and 134,000,000 in South Asia compared to 106,700,000 in 1980. That's phenomenal growth for which we must pause and thank the Lord God. It is estimated that the professing Christian population of Korea is 30 percent of the total population.

But let's not be fooled by Christian strength in the wildfire regions of the world. In general, population growth is exceeding Christian growth and our earlier ambitious projections of evangelizing the world by the year 2000 are ebbing away with each passing year, ebbing away into the reality that we are losing the battle.

Every minute of every day China's population increases by 30 Chinese babies, a population increase of 17,000,000 annually. A government study says there are 1,133,682,581 permanent residents in China today, that's 20,000,000 more than previously estimated. Women of child-bearing years now comprise more than a fourth of China's people. Despite the fact that 11,000,000 abortions are performed in China every year, the population continues to explode .[8]

While population growth is not as acute worldwide, we should never be tempted to compare our missionary efforts today with last year or a decade ago. We should always compare our efforts with the reality of what must be done, not what has been done.

Our goals have been smashed in the past and it appears they continue to be smashed today. The efforts of the A.D. 2000 movement may change all that, but changing the patterns of history is always an uphill battle.

Currently we are losing the battle on several fronts. What are they?

First, we are losing the battle in personnel. Are there more missionaries than the world needs? The average American pastor might be tempted to answer in the affirmative when he considers the steady stream of mission candidates begging for an opportunity to present their work in his church. But we must look at the world's need, not the pastor's dilemma.

Some mission strategists in the know estimate that it takes one missionary couple about 15 years to learn the language and culture of their field, sow the seed faithfully, and plant a growing, vibrant church among a group of 5,000 people. At that rate, David Bryant estimated in 1984 that it would take 600,000 more missionaries to complete the task of world evangelization by A.D. 2000.[9] It should not come as a shock that we are way behind that pace.

We are losing the battle on another front. Insufficient missionaries means insufficient converts to Christ, and consequently insufficient new missionaries to accomplish world evangelization. With all the excellent reports coming out of Africa, South America and Asia, and with a TV evangelist on every channel and a church on every corner in America, it's difficult to appreciate that there are areas of the world with little or no Christians at all. But there are many such areas.

For example, in 1989 less than one percent of Japan's population of

123,231,000 were Christians. With a population of 55,377,000 Turkey has only about 100 Christians. And, of course, the recent crisis in the Persian Gulf brought a great deal of the world face to face with just how closed a society can be to the gospel when it is dominated by Islam.

There are still 5,390 unreached languages in the world, languages which have no Bible.[10] The unreached peoples of the world are categorized into 16,750 people groups. These groups represent 59 percent of the world's population.[11] We are losing the battle.

A third front on which the battle wages fiercely but badly is in churches planted. By informed estimates, the missionary enterprise needs to plant 6,000,000 new churches (one for every 1,000 people) by the end of the century if we are going to reach the 6 billion non-Christians who will be alive in the year A.D. 2000.[12]

Although the number of missionaries is insufficient, there is another factor that spells potential defeat. With a local New Testament church functioning in Christ's design as the ultimate end of mission work, you would think that the vast majority of missionary personnel are church planters. You'd think that, but you'd be wrong. One veteran missionary analyst estimates that only 28 percent of missionaries around the world are directly involved in church planting.[13]

The need for planting churches is, of course, not the only need in missions. Nevertheless it is a genuine and overwhelming need. Still, the missionary force is primarily involved in other pursuits. What is the major activity of today's missionaries? Donald McGavran stated that 80 percent of all foreign missionary activity involves social work.[14] As important as social work is, because the hungry need to be fed and the homeless need shelter, by themselves these do not win the war we wage against the gates of hell.

There is another front on which we are losing the battle. It is the statistical front. Allow me to explain.

Mark Twain had some pertinent things to say about statistics, listing them as one of three categories of lies. We all know that any impression can be created with facts and figures. I am doing that right now. I want you to understand that as impressive as the reports are from the wildfire regions of the world, and there have been increases in the last few years in the number of people giving their lives to missions, these figures pale into insignificance when compared with the number of non-Christians and the need for additional missions personnel.

While the statistics which indicate that we are losing the battle do not tell the whole story, neither do the statistics which make us feel good about the battle. One of my great concerns at the threshold of the 21st century is that we will believe our own statistics. Let me give you an example.

American evangelicals became excited when they read the headlines in *Christianity Today* a few years ago (October 7, 1983) which said, "In Africa, 16,400 People Became Christians Today." But these statistics need some examination. The good folks at the Missions Advanced Research Communication Center (MARC) undertook the examination.

"This is but one of hundreds of items appearing regularly in the evangelical press that fosters the idea that evangelization, as fervently desired by evangelicals, is making impressive strides. What the report did not make clear, however, is that: (1) 12,560 of the 16,400 are babies born into Christian homes. This is growth that merely keeps pace with population growth. (2) Of the 3,840 actual conversions occurring daily, only about 750 are related to evangelical groups. About half are Roman Catholic, and the remainder become members of African indigenous groups, American sects, the Orthodox church, or other non-evangelical groups."[15] While we must pause to thank God for those 750 who came to Christ, we must also sense that we are losing the battle.

"In Africa, 16,400 people became Christians today"*

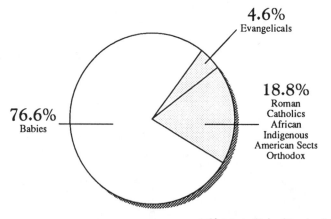

4.6%
Evangelicals

18.8%
Roman
Catholics
African
Indigenous
American Sects
Orthodox

76.6%
Babies

* *Christianity Today* (October 7, 1983)

Another front on which the battle is being lost is in the established church. Many of the statistics relating to world Christians and church members represent those who are afflicted with a disease called "nominalism." Nominalism means a person belongs to the church but has little contact with it. That these people are really saved is questionable.

Although the scene of a major part of Christian history, Great Britain and Europe are infested with nominalism. In Britain church attendance continues to decline (about 2 percent a year). The Church of England claims to have 30,000,000 baptized members, but the church reports less than 2,000,000 active members and less than 750,000 Anglicans attend church on any given Sunday.[16] Oh, well, that's the Anglicans. Perhaps evangelicals expect it. But half of England's Methodist churches have less than 25 in attendance on a typical Sunday.

Europe today has been accurately described as being a secular post-Christian society. More than a third of Europeans overall do not believe in God. A recent poll for the European Community indicated that southern Europeans tend to be more pious than their northern counterparts. While the total number of Christians in Europe rose slightly since 1980 from 403,000,000 to almost 408,000,000 in 1988, most of that growth came from Eastern and not Western Europe. France is 74 percent Roman Catholic, though only 6 percent are practicing Catholics. Sweden is 60 percent Lutheran with only 3-4 percent practicing.[17] About 92 percent of Norway's 4,200,000 people are members of the Church of Norway, confirmed and baptized in the church, but only 3 percent attend church on Sunday. That's not winning the battle.

One final front on which the battle is being lost, and thus our ambitious goals are currently appearing to be smashed, is the number of "Christians" leaving the faith. I didn't say leaving the church; many have already done that without official notification. I said they are leaving the faith.

In 1979, 1,815,100 adult Christians in Europe abandoned the church to become agnostics, atheists or adherents of non-Christian religions. North America also registered a net decline of almost 1,000,000 "Christians."[18] Things have gotten worse since then.

In the United States a 1990 Gallup poll asked Americans to indicate their religious preference. "None" jumped to 9 percent from 2 percent in 1952.

About a decade after I graduated from college, my history professor at the Christian college I attended "converted" to Judaism. He had presumably become a Messianic Jew earlier in his life, one who came from darkness to light, but now he had opted to return to the darkness. I couldn't understand it at the time. Now I have learned that he is not alone.

The goals of evangelizing the entire world by the end of this century, established a decade or more ago, were grandiose indeed. But, in full respect to those who established these goals, they were also unrealistic. Now such goals are being intensified with the approach of the new millennium. If previously we were unsuccessful with more time until the dawn of A.D. 2000, I wonder what makes us think we will be successful with less time? Our goals have been stated, but so far they have been smashed.

Jim Engel and Jerry Jones published a 1989 report entitled Boomers and the Future of World Missions. Their sobering conclusion statement was: "A generation of American Christians has given obediently and generously. Unfortunately, they have aged and are now mostly beyond 55. Here is a conclusion which cannot be ignored: It is highly unlikely that this aging financial base in North America can support accelerated world evangelization. It is obvious that the slack must be taken up by younger Christians, especially those born since World War II. Many ambitious AD 2000 programs will end up in wreckage unless boomer interest can be captured."[19]

Now, put all the statistics behind you. Conflicting figures are always available. Conflicting assessments of the success of winning the world to Christ by A.D. 2000 are advanced by mission strategists. Many will dispute my conclusions here. But, if you really want to see what the potential for missionary success in the next decade is, remember Engel and Jones' conclusion: "Our missionary success in the near future (excluding the miraculous intervention of God) depends largely on an outpouring of financial support from Baby Boomers." Scary, isn't it?

Regardless of what the preachers of prosperity, the prophets of millennial bliss, or the overly optimistic strategists say, the battle is raging and we are not winning. The archenemy has more soldiers and more resources than we have. In fact, the only thing we have going for us is our Commander-in-Chief.

But I am not pessimistic, even though there is good evidence around us to foster pessimism. My lack of pessimism may be attributed to remembering Moses' charge to the Israelites just before he died. The great leader said, "When thou goest out to battle against thine enemies, and seest horses, and chariots, and a people more than thou, be not afraid of them: for the LORD thy God is with thee" (Deut. 20:1).

Our hope is in the Lord, but we must match that hope with a change in some fundamental attitudes about life, some fundamental changes in spending patterns, if we are to win the world to Christ. That's what this book is all about.

– 3 –

America as a Sending Nation

As *if it* weren't enough that the church is essentially not winning the battle around the world, there is even more crushing news, for most Americans at least.

We Americans have always thought of ourselves as the staging ground for world evangelism. We are the great sending nation. We are not a mission field; we are a sending field. If the world is not being evangelized as we had hoped, it certainly isn't our fault. It must be England's fault or Europe's fault.

But is that really true? Is it possible that another country sends more of its sons and daughters into the harvest fields than does the United States? Per capita, is there any other nation that provides more missionaries to the world than does the USA?

The answer will shock most American Christians. Although it is true that the lion's share of missionaries (presently 40,221 career and 30,221 short term) still come from the USA, yet per capita America is not the leader in sending her sons and daughters abroad. According to the 13th edition of the Mission Handbook, the "bible" of missionary analysis, America ranks 16th per capita in the list of countries sending missionaries overseas. That's right. Sixteenth! In ratio to the national population, America ranks behind Ireland, Belgium, Spain, Netherlands,

Portugal, Italy, Canada, France, Switzerland, New Zealand, Norway, West Germany, Australia and Sweden.[20]

Now, let's stop and take a breath. And while we do, let's analyze what this means. Canada and 14 European nations were significantly ahead of the USA in the number of missionaries per capita sent overseas. Of 20 Western nations, America, the "Christian" nation, ranked 16th (see chart on page 27).

American Christians should take note of what nations bettered the USA. When we think of Switzerland, we think of skiing, chocolate and the beauty of the Alps. We think of bankers and watchmakers. We do not think of missionaries. But Switzerland did twice as well as America in sending missionaries overseas.

Canadians can look with some degree of satisfaction to the fact that Canada also did twice as well as America in this area. The Dutch church in the Netherlands, usually more Calvinistic than her American counterparts, had a ratio of one missionary for ever 1,313 people. That's nearly four times the ratio of the USA. America's ratio was one missionary for every 4,780 Americans (a 1990 report puts the USA ratio at one in 3,500).

Even Sweden, secular Sweden, a country not known for its conservatism or strict moral code, did better than America. Ahead of everyone else, however, was Ireland with one missionary for every 328 people in its population.

Listen, Christian America. We are not doing the job we think we are. Although there are 70,969 missions personnel serving overseas from the USA, the church in America is not keeping pace with many other nations of the world in per capita sending to the regions beyond.

Consider this. In 1988 there were 35,900 Protestant non-Western missionaries in the world. There are presently 1,094 non-Western mission agencies.[21] If the battle is being lost around the world, we Americans must be careful not to point fingers. Our record is impressive, but comparatively becoming less impressive all the time, especially when we consider our population and the fact that the American church is probably the wealthiest in the world.

How are we really doing? Well, we are behind some countries you would not expect. But if we take consolation in that someone is doing the job even if America isn't, we shouldn't. If you have been waiting for the other shoe to drop, here it is.

Although it may be surprising that America ranks so low per capita among sending nations, it may be more surprising that more than 90 percent of the missionaries sent out by the 15 Western nations ahead of the USA were Roman Catholic missionaries.[22] Surprised? Don't be. Look at the nations that rank ahead of the USA. Belgium, Spain, Portugal, Italy and France, none of which are Protestant strongholds.

PER CAPITA PERCENTAGE OF NATIONAL MISSIONARIES

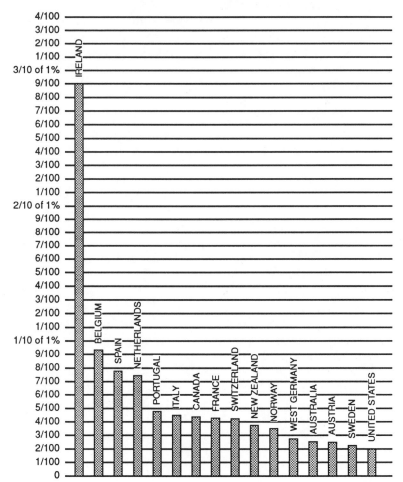

The bottom line is this. Although their populations may be less, many other nations are sending more of their sons and daughters per capita overseas as missionaries than is the United States. And further, the vast majority of those sent out by these nations are Roman Catholic missionaries. How are we really doing, America? Are we winning the battle? Judge for yourself.

– 4 –

America as a Mission Field

Why is America not the sending nation we expected it to be? Well, that's what this book is all about. But one reason is clear.

The American church is not as strong a missionary sending body as it could be because the American church is not as strong as it could be. In fact, the mission field in our own backyard is so overwhelming that the American church cannot set its sights on the world as it ought.

America, a mission field? No, it can't be. We are so strong, so civilized. We have so many religious radio and television programs (13,500,000 Americans watch TV ministries each week). We have so many Bible conferences and Christian resorts. We have so many churches. We have so many Christian colleges and seminaries. America is not a mission field. It can't be.

Perhaps in the air-conditioned comfort of our attractively decorated churches it is difficult to envision America as a mission field. Perhaps as we American Christians receive daily doses of mail advertising Christian book clubs, tape cassettes, videos, one-day seminars, and Caribbean cruises with our favorite Christian recording artists, it is difficult to believe that America is a mission field. Difficult? Yes. Impossible? The facts say otherwise.

How are we really doing — in America?

The State of America

America. By the very word, pride wells up in the hearts of most Americans. America is the country whose coins are stamped, "In God We Trust." It is the country whose President takes the oath of office with one hand raised and the other on the Bible. It is the country so concerned with religious freedom that the first amendment to the United States Constitution provides that "Congress shall make no law respecting an establishment of religion, or prohibiting the free exercise thereof. . . ."

The Puritans and Pilgrims came to this great land seeking religious freedom, freedom to worship and serve God as they saw fit. Early schools were very religious in nature. Prayer was offered to God at the beginning of each class. Churches played a central role in the life of American towns.

But that was America then; this is America now. At the turn of the last century it was estimated that two out of every three Americans were born-again, Bible-believing Christians.[23] That isn't true today. In fact, Donald McGavran estimated there are 30,000,000 hard-core pagans in America who are anti-Christian.[24] Religious freedom is still guaranteed, but with more than 169,000,000 unchurched people in America, we have failed to practice that freedom and thus have become more and more secular and irreligious.

Christian influence in America has waned to such an extent that everything which remotely appears to be "religious" is either outlawed, downplayed or scorned. Prayer in public school has been ruled unconstitutional. On the other hand, pornography is constitutional because the justices of our land cannot determine what it is. The only mention of prayer in the schools today is the graffiti on the wall that says, "In case of a nuclear attack, the ban on prayer will be lifted."

Nativity scenes are being removed from public property because they are offensive to the secular majority. The AIDS crisis is approached with prevention techniques which never address morality. This is the mission field — America, where homosexuals have rights but creationists do not.

Add to the secular majority the phenomenal growth of other religions in America. Islam and Hinduism, most specifically, have been making much greater inroads into the Christian stronghold of America than Christians have been making into traditional Muslim or Hindu strongholds.

Over a million visitors are expected to attend the next Cultural Festival of India to be held in New York City. *Hinduism Today* says, "It follows on the heels of three earlier festivals, two in India and one in England. The 1985 England festival was credited with permanently improving the public image of Hinduism in the United Kingdom, the same goal as the upcoming American festival."

I was preaching in Chicago and needed to get to the airport in a hurry. I left Moody Church, ran into the street, and hailed a taxi. As we sped off toward O'Hare, I engaged the cabbie in conversation and learned he was a Muslim. En route to the airport we passed a huge building which had been converted into a mosque. I asked him if he attended there for prayer and he said that he did, twice a day. When I inquired how many men attended the daily services he said, "The 4:00 p.m. service usually has about 1,500 worshippers. The 4:00 a.m. service is not as well attended, only around 900."

Can you imagine getting 900 Baptists, Methodists, Pentecostals, Presbyterians, or other American Christians to a 4:00 a.m. prayer service, every morning?

The State of America's Churches

According to the 1990 edition of the *Yearbook of American and Canadian Churches*, a total of 145,383,738 or 58.7 percent of the population belonged to a church, a synagogue, or some other religious organization in 1989. There are 343,000 churches in America[25] claiming a membership of 130,000,000 people. That sounds impressive, but dissecting this statistic does not generate confidence in the healthy state of the evangelical church in America. Of these churches, 23,500 are Roman Catholic; 6,900 churches are Mormon; 6,000 churches are Jehovah's Witnesses' Kingdom Halls; 5,000 churches are actually Jewish synagogues; and 1,600 are the Orthodox Church.[26]

Of the 70,000,000 Protestants in the United States, over 42,000,000 belong to churches associated with the National Council of Churches and would not ordinarily be considered evangelical.[27] Thus, the number of churches in the USA which can be launching pads for the gospel is not as large as we may think.

Moreover, many American churches are not healthy. It is estimated that 80-85 percent of American churches have plateaued or are declining.[28] Only 20 percent of all American churches have an average attendance of more than 200 people. Sunday school watcher Elmer

Towns says that the average church has only 87 people in Sunday school attendance. A 1990 report in *Pulpit Helps* indicated that in 1980 there were 196,237 Sunday schools in the USA with a total enrollment of 35,639,788. In 1988 there were only 112,197 Sunday schools in the USA with a total enrollment of 27,210,060, a decrease of 8,429,718 in just eight years. In America, the Sunday school movement is dying. On Sunday morning you can find more Americans on any golf course than in the average American church.

What is worse, the number of churches in America is not growing. In 1900 there were 27 churches for every 10,000 Americans. In 1985 this figure had declined so drastically that it is painful to report. There are now only 12 churches for every 10,000 Americans, less than half the former amount.[29] Yes, this is the day of the super church, but even the phenomenon of the super church cannot account for this decline.

Add to this the number of churches that are now closing. There are over 66,000 closed churched in America. Another 62,000 are presently without pastors.[30] Between 3,500 and 4,000 churches close their doors each year in the USA.[31]

Are we a mission field?

And one final thing. These statistics represent church membership in America. No one reading these figures is foolish enough to believe that church membership is the same as church involvement. Pollster George Gallup reported in May 1975 that 68 percent of Americans are members of a church or synagogue.[32] But before we rejoice at this percentage, we ought to realize this is only one percent above the all-time record low for church membership in America. Remember, the percentage is only 58.7 percent in the 1990 edition of the *Yearbook of American and Canadian Churches*. As bad as these numbers may appear, they probably paint a much rosier picture than the actual health of the church, especially with regard to garnering and sending missionaries overseas.

How are we really doing? We will do only as well as the home base does, and in many places the home base has plateaued. How are we really doing? We are not doing as well at home as it may appear on Sunday morning, and this impacts how we are doing around the world.

Once while pleading with a group of pastors to keep their eyes open for young men whom they could influence toward ministry, one pastor replied to me, "America is already overchurched. Every time a pastor resigns, the church receives dozens, even hundreds of unsolicited resumes from men who are interested in pastoring that church. There is a glut of men in the ministry."

A couple of years ago I saw an alumni ballot from a large seminary in America. The ballot was for alumni to choose two from their ranks, a male and a female, as alumni board representatives. The two male candidates each had earned the M.Div. degree, the usual ministry degree. One of the female candidates had earned the M.R.E. degree and the other the M.Div. All had been seminary trained for professional ministry, lifetime ministry. However, although one of the female candidates was involved in women's ministries, the other was listed as a homemaker. And the two men? One was a U.S. attorney and the other a bank executive. It would appear that the "glut of men in the ministry" may have been a bit overstated.

America is not overchurched. It may be oversupplied with disgruntled pastors seeking greener pastures or returning from a hiatus from their calling, but it is not overchurched. A total of 169,000,000 unaffiliated and unchurched Americans constitutes a vast mission field.[33]

In 1900, 66 percent of the American population belonged to Bible-believing, soul-winning churches. They all professed faith in Christ as Saviour. Yet it is predicted that by the year 2000 there will only be 33 percent of the American population who belong to church.[34] Overchurched? I don't think so!

The sending nation, the launching pad for world evangelization, has itself become a vast mission field with a severely weakened operational base.

Conclusion

The Western world is so data oriented, so trivia crazed, so statistics inundated that it is difficult for us to appreciate facts and figures anymore. This is why I pray the preceding will be more than meaningless numbers to you. I pray that I have conveyed a sense of need, a sense of urgency, and that you will demonstrate a willingness to take a second look at how things really are.

Although the Christian church has existed for 20 centuries encompassing many generations, none has ever really won its entire generation to the Lord. But at least we have had an army of soldiers ready to do battle against Satan.

Now it appears the recruiting officers for the army of Christ are being unheeded, muzzled, if not silenced in some places. While the battle is going badly and more soldiers are desperately needed, still fewer and fewer solders, in proportion to the population, are enlisting for lifetime ministry. This spells trouble on the horizon, and the troops are by and large unaware of the latest intelligence reports.

One thing cannot be denied. Our generation is alone responsible to win this generation to the Lord. Our generation alone has opportunity to do so. If you and I lose this battle, we will not lose the war. But we will lose one generation, and that's a loss in which the casualty count is too high.

Our missions goals, born out of the cleanliness of theory, have been smashed in the past by the mess of reality. Our home base, although still the chief source of missions money and missions personnel, is seriously lagging behind its potential on both scores. In fact, the launching pad for world evangelism has itself become a worthy target for Two Thirds World missionaries.

The truth is that while the number of career missionaries, lifetime missionaries, the USA sends overseas continues to increase, the number of career missionaries to short termers continues to decline, 57 percent of the total today, down from 64 percent of the total in 1985.[35] Are we headed for a short term, part time missionary force? If we are, we're headed for disaster. Our Lord did not call His disciples to go into all the world and preach the gospel part time, or for a short term. Lifetime was His intent, and lifetime was His command.

The harvest fields have more souls to be harvested today than ever before, and the number of laborers in ratio to those needy souls is smaller than ever before. In business, that's a classic formula for bankruptcy.

The fact is we are not getting the job done and we need more help. The fact is we are getting further behind every day and we need more help. The fact is Satan constantly makes significant gains into the lives of those who form the base for world missions and we need more help.

The ministry is vanishing before our eyes. The bottom line is, we need more help! We need you.

Part Two
The Devilish Diversion

How did we get where we are?

The Devilish Diversion

How did we get where we are?

Every road leads somewhere, even if only to a dead end. By watching for signs and natural landmarks along the way, we can pretty well tell where the road is headed.

The same is true with the road that brought us to increased demand for laborers and dwindling supplies of the same. How did we get where we are?

Let's be fair. No one planned for us to be in this situation. Well, almost no one. That old snake, Lucifer, had this in mind all along. His master plan has been clear from the start. If he couldn't get God's soldiers to defect, he had to get them diverted from what was most important to their Commander-in-Chief. His plan worked.

From the chapters that follow it will be evident that Satan did not use a rifle to shoot at God's army; rather, he used a shotgun. He attacked on every front; he shot at every soldier. We did not get in this mess by one person letting down his guard. Satan knew that wouldn't work. He needed to create simultaneous diversions that would capture the attention of the whole army, not just a few.

What are the causes of decreased army recruits? What makes more and more soldiers want to serve a hitch and then muster out rather than be a career soldier? What kinds of people, good people, soldiers themselves permit the devil to divert them so that the ministry vanishes before our eyes? Let's investigate some of them.

37

– 5 –

Secular Self-Interest

You see them everywhere. They drive Volvos, Saabs, BMWs. They wear pinstriped wool suits or expensive dresses. They work for corporate America in high-rise office buildings glimmering of glass and steel. They are today's young Turks in the business world. There is only one thing different about many of them — their names.

They aren't called Tom, Dick or Harry. They don't answer to Mary, Elizabeth or Jean. They have funny names, names like Wyoming, Autumn, Cinnamon or Fawn. They are the children of the flower children. They are the offspring of the protesters of the 60s. They were born in communes and named after things like flowers and twigs.

Others were born into middle class homes. They grew up in church but felt their parents were old fashioned and their pastor a little out of touch. Their names may have been more traditional, but their direction in life was still the same.

Many of today's young people are interested in things much different from what interested their parents. They have no major wars to protest.

They are not as cause-oriented as their fathers and mothers. They are not as idealistic. They see clearly what happened to their parents' ideals. They understand their parents' lives to have been megajumps from maternity ward to marches on Washington to money on Wall Street. Disillusioned, many young people today have decided to cut out the middle man and the middle jump.

New heroes have emerged on television, heroes who have become role models. Today's modern college students have not been raised on Beaver Cleaver but on Alex P. Keaton. They are well dressed, in control of themselves, articulate and have one goal in life — to make money.

This trend toward secular self-interest is not entirely new. We have always looked out for Number One. But never has the trend been so blatant. Never before have Christian young people had the freedom to be so vocal about their life's number one goal — to make money.

Several years ago at Christmas, during a Sunday evening service, the youth pastor invited some of the college students who were home for the holidays to tell how things were going at school. There was the usual assortment of accounting majors, business majors and undecideds in the group. But one young man gave testimony that caught my ear.

This fellow had gone to a Christian university to prepare for some kind of ministry. He had completed two years at this university when he decided to drop out and join the Navy. To the church congregation assembled that night he unashamedly announced that the reason he entered the Navy was that here he "would be trained in the field of electronics where he could make big bucks in a career" after he was out. That's a classic example of secular self-interest.

Although we expect this kind of reasoning from the world, I have difficulty adjusting my thinking that it should be acceptable in the church.

Is there something wrong with Christian men and women aspiring to a career in business? Absolutely not! If there were, I know a great number of godly business people who are out of the will of God. No, there is no dishonor in making money, especially if the Christian businessman is faithful to the Lord with his resources. I have often said, with tongue in cheek, that profit is not without honor.

But college students today have grown up in a world filled with perks, a healthy stock market and benefit packages. So much have these things permeated our society that I have had innumerable pulpit committees lament to me that young pastors are more frequently asking only one question when being considered for a pulpit position, "How much?"

Because of this prevalent attitude of secular self-interest many Christian colleges have adapted to meet the demand. Since students want to make money, why not teach them how? Therefore, in many Christian colleges today the number one major is business. In fact, some colleges once known for the quality and quantity of pastors and missionaries they graduated are now inhabited by one-third to one-half business majors.

Since careers of this type are being sought by Christian college students in growing numbers, there doesn't seem to be any reason to key college advertising to anything else. In a recent edition of *Campus Life*[1] magazine, an evangelical magazine that keeps its finger on the pulse of young America, I noticed that the college ads all looked strangely alike. Every ad, not just one or two, but every ad fell into one of the following categories: general, nursing, psychology, computer science, accounting or business. There was not a single ad for any specific kind of ministry.

Why is this? Because most of today's young people exhibit little interest in sacrificing their goals for the goal of world evangelism. Perhaps the rapid and overwhelming increase of majors in accounting, business, computer science, etc. reflects one of two things. Either Christian young people have captured a healthy awareness that they are to be the salt of the earth, infiltrating every area of life, or else Christian young people have finally succumbed to the temptation to hang up the ministry enterprise and just make money like everybody else.

The stigma is finally gone. No longer do Christian college students have to include lifetime ministry in their career considerations. They can admit to their parents without shame, "I want to make money like everybody else."

The honest truth is that they just want to be left alone. They want to live out the great American dream. They want to get married, have a family, a nice car, a big house and a job that pays them a lot of money. They admit that they are little interested in exploring what God may have for them. They want the good life, what is best for them.

Whereas their parents at this age turned their interests outward toward world causes, many of today's young people have discerned the futility of their parents' efforts. They have seen the evolution of their parents' movement orientation to money orientation, and today's young people have decided that their parents have finally found peace — in an IRA.

Young Christian, if everything you enjoy for all eternity is judged acceptable and awarded at the judgment seat of Christ, and if this is the only life you have in which to lay up treasures in heaven, then to spend all your time, all your talent, all your money for the seventy years of this world and spend none of it working for the next isn't silly—it's stupid! Remember, dear friend, you never see a hearse with a U–Haul attached. You can't take it with you, but you can send it on ahead!

The devil has diverted an increasing number of talented young Christians into legitimate professions. But in so doing he has craftily reduced the pool of candidates for lifetime service to the Lord of Glory. Many of today's bright Christian college students have allowed what is good to rob them of what is best.

– 6 –

Upward Mobility Parents

As *if today's* youth didn't have enough to contend with in the growing tendency toward secular self-interest, they must deal also with upwardly mobile parents. Rather than check the self-interest of their children, these parents contribute to it. That's how we got where we are in the vanishing ministry.

Upward mobility is that tendency to progress upward in a spiraling fashion from where we are to where we want to be. In the case of many parents stuck in careers with no future, this upward mobility must be lived out in the lives and careers of their children.

Let's face it! Who of us as parents wants our children to have less than we had? Who of us wants our children to go through the struggles we went through? Probably none of us. And it's this very sentiment, a wholesome and legitimate one, that causes the upward mobility syndrome.

Parents are willing to do just about anything to soften the crash of reality into the lives of their children. We want to spare them the agony of "making it on their own" the way we had to. So we push them. We push them upward in every area of life.

My family and I live in a modest home. It's far less expensive than those across my back fence. We care for it well, cut the grass and trim the hedge as a testimony to the Lord and out of a sense of wholesome pride. We have a nice house, adequate for our needs. But it wasn't always this way. I'm sure it's the same with every parent reading this.

The first apartment my wife and I had after we were married was in a college town. I was finishing my bachelor's degree at the time. We lived above a dear little old lady who was extremely hard of hearing. Our apartment consisted of a living room, a tiny bedroom and an even smaller bathroom. We had to share the kitchen with our landlady downstairs. We even shared the refrigerator — she had two shelves and we had two shelves. My wife did light housework, and I maintained the property in general. Both of us cared for the well-being of our hard-of-hearing landlady. We paid five dollars a week in rent.

Ah, the good old days. They bring back great memories, don't they? Fighting off the neighbor's dog every time I took out the trash. Freezing each winter night because insufficient heat got upstairs through those old, rusty pipes. Finding that our landlady had eaten our supper by mistake. Those were great days. You probably think I'd return to them in a minute. Not on your life!

Those days make great memories and equally great stories, but the greatest thing about them is that they are past forever. I like owning my own home. I like regulating my own heat. I like taking out my own trash (that may be an overstatement). I don't want to return to the good old days.

It's this very sense of thankfulness that causes parents to shield their children from the hardships they had to endure. It's this desire that propels us into the upward mobility syndrome.

Innocent as it may appear, upward mobility can turn ugly in a hurry. It can cause irreparable damage to the cause of Christ without most parents even knowing it.

Where does parental upward mobility for their children most clearly evidence itself? In the related areas of education and profession. Our upward mobility is seen in the advice Christian parents give their children with regard to where to go to college and what major to choose.

In an address I delivered to graduates of my alma mater, I cautioned those pastors and missionaries present to be careful about how they portrayed their alma mater to their children. It is devastating to a teenager's image of his parents to hear them say, "My school was good enough for me, but I want something better for you." I suggested that it was likely some of those pastors present had said something similar to their sons and had actually driven them from lifetime ministry to secular employment.

Within one half hour after my address was finished, the Dean of Students at that institution had one of the most prestigious alumni, a respected pastor, in his office in tears. He said, "I did exactly what Dr. Kroll said. I thought my alma mater wasn't good enough for my son and so I sent him off to the university and I've lost him forever." Upward mobility parents, especially those involved in lifetime ministry, are deadly forces contributing to the vanishing ministry.

Dr. James Dobson said, "Sometimes we're so concerned to give our children what we never had while growing up, we neglect to give them what we did have while growing up."

Upward mobility among parents is evident not only in the colleges and universities to which Christians send their children but also in the careers they encourage their children to enter.

When a Christian dad sits down with his Christian son to talk about the future, usually the conversation runs something like this. "Well, son, you need to think about your future. You need to consider job security, pension plans, the possibility of advancement. You ought to check out the new hi tech fields. There's a lot of money to be made in them. You'll be able to take good care of your family."

Although all of this sounds like good advice, and although it is all too frequently the sum and substance of those fatherly chats about careers, there is something dreadfully wrong about all this. The whole conversation centers around the son's ability to live in this world when it is much more important that he know how to live for the next. Somehow the conversation has gotten off center. It ought to include singing a chorus or two of "This world is not my home, I'm just a'passin' through. My treasures are laid up, somewhere beyond the blue."

Our children receive the best counsel from us when we advise them to choose a career that will enhance their ability to serve the Lord, not themselves and their own self-interest. This chosen career may not pay as well as some others, but it sure beats being an eternal pauper. This is unlikely to be the case, however, when all around us we see upwardly mobile parents struggling to give their sons and daughters more than they had so that the next generation can make a good living.

The trouble with all this is that even Christian upward mobility parents seem to prefer that their children enter a career which pays well, one in which they can settle down and pursue their secular self-interest. The challenge to ministry is a non-challenge. It doesn't exist.

Perhaps the challenge to ministry doesn't exist in career talk because many Christian parents perceive that if they commit their children to God, He will cruelly force them to live in poverty and deprivation all their lives in some far-off, infested jungle. Or worse, they won't experience the glamour of being sent to the field but will experience the horror of being tucked away as pastor and wife in a little church in a no-name town best described as "ten miles south of resume speed."

Upward mobility parents have always believed that if they worked hard their children wouldn't have to, but they certainly never believed their children would ruin their lives by uprooting their grandchildren and moving them to some non-grandparently place. Ministry may require this of their children, and even Christian parents want little or nothing to do with that,

The devil's diversion in the minds of upward mobility parents is to shield their children from the hardship of denial. In fact, the Lord Jesus seems to indicate just the opposite when He says, "Whosoever will come after me, let him deny himself, and take up his cross, and follow me. For whosoever will save his life shall lose it; but whosoever shall lose his life for my sake and the gospel's, the same shall save it. For what shall it profit a man, if he shall gain the whole world and lose his own soul?" (Mark 8:34-36).

Parents, your children, like mine, are treasures. It is certainly not wrong for us to want God's very best for them. But we bear a responsibility, like Hannah in the Old Testament and Eunice in the New Testament, to give our children to God. After all, why do we go through that cute little baby dedication service in our churches if when it comes time to consider a career we attempt to shield them from lifetime ministry?

You need not worry about the welfare of your children when you give them to God. He can take better care of them than they can of themselves. You need not worry about the career advancement of your children when you give them to God. After all, He is the captain of a mighty army, the potter over every piece of clay. You need not worry about giving your children in lifetime ministry to God. If He doesn't want to use them in this way, He'll give them back to business, industry, education or another career.

But upward mobility parents think they know better than God what is right for their children. After all, they got their information from Dow Jones or the *Wall Street Journal.* Christian upward mobility parents are Christians with a small "c," but they are capitalists with a large "C." With regard to their children, they have fallen to the devil's diversion.

Dad and Mom, the greatest denial you can make to your children is not the denial of food or shelter. It isn't even the denial of your time or your love. The greatest denial you can make to your children is to deny them from being your greatest gift to God. Don't dedicate them to God at birth and direct them from Him at college or career time!

If we must be upwardly mobile parents, let's make sure that this mobility will carry our children far beyond the top of the World Trade Towers. Let's insure that this upward mobility will carry our children all the way to the third heaven. Give your children to God and lifetime ministry. If He chooses to give them back, receive them with the same joy as if He kept them.

– 7 –

WAGAPS Elementary Teachers

There aren't many people I admire more than Christian school teachers. Most of them are overworked and underpaid. They are somebody special.

I am an advocate of Christian education, from cradle to grave. My four children have all come up through the Christian school system. Two of them have already graduated from a Christian high school. Although I do not believe that the worst Christian school is better than the best public school, I do applaud the efforts of Christian educators to teach in a total Christian environment.

I also applaud the efforts of Christian educators who remain in the public school system. Many of them have greater Christian influence on their students than some teachers in Christian schools. For some of their students, they are the only Christian influence these teenagers will ever have. They are to be commended.

The Christian school movement has come a long way in the last quarter of a century. Many schools are flourishing with fully equipped laboratories, modern gymnasiums, full athletic programs. Still, something is missing.

Some of the greatest influences on teenagers have consistently missed the most wonderful opportunities to incline our teens toward ministry. These great influences are Christian school teachers.

Over the years as a college professor I have watched freshmen with great interest and considerable amusement. I have chuckled at their ineptitude; I have cried at the same thing. But having taught twenty years in Christian colleges and universities, I have always wondered why it should be that there was no discernible difference in commitment to the Lord between those freshmen who entered from Christian schools and those freshmen who entered from public schools.

It has also been my responsibility over the years to administer Bible comprehensive exams to incoming students, exams to test their general Bible knowledge. I have wondered why it should be that there was no discernible difference in Bible knowledge between those freshmen who entered from Christian schools and those freshmen who entered from public schools.

But perhaps that which has caused the most wonder to me is why I have never been able to trace the trail that leads to ministry back to the Christian school. I have wondered why it should be that there was no discernible difference in commitment to ministry between those freshmen who entered college from Christian high schools and those freshmen who entered college from public high schools.

Why does the path from Christian elementary education, which leads so naturally to Christian secondary education, not lead so naturally to Christian post-secondary education? Why does the young man or woman who has been raised in the church and educated in the Christian school not more frequently build on that base for a life of ministry?

There are no pat answers. But there are some observations to be made. One observation is what I call the WAGAPS Christian school teacher. The WAGAPS teacher appears to be concerned, and rightly so, with the quality of education being provided by the Christian school he serves. He seems to make his courses a little tougher, he piles on the homework a little higher, he makes the demands on his students a little stiffer. He is a difficult grader and is always saying things like, "Your education in this class is far superior to what those kids in the public schools are getting. You are years ahead of them."

And, oh yes, in his effort to provide a superior education, the WAGAPS Christian school teacher drives his students as far from lifetime ministry as possible. Without intending to do so, this teacher has helped us get where we are in the vanishing ministry.

Whatever spiritual lessons the WAGAPS teacher attempts to teach his students are smothered by his incessant need to be professional, to be tough, to be better than the public school. Hence, the WAGAPS teacher teaches subjects; he does not teach students. He educates; he does not influence.

In case you haven't guessed, WAGAPS is an acronym for "We're As Good As Public Schools." It describes the teacher, man or woman, who has become so preoccupied with the profession of teaching that he has forgotten the privilege of the Christian teacher. He is professional all right, but many of his students need him to be more pastoral and parental than professional.

Few people have the influence on teenagers today that good teachers have. Few teachers have greater opportunity to influence Christian young people toward lifetime ministry than Christian school teachers have. Yet, apparently, few people utilize this opportunity so infrequently.

I have had the delightful privilege of being the commencement speaker at many Christian high school graduations each year. I always asked for a few minutes alone with the seniors. I wanted to learn what influences had brought them to this stage in their life.

Several years ago I addressed a large Christian high school in a southern state. There were 76 students in the graduating class. That should tell you something about the size of this school. When I asked the graduates some questions about their future, I was shocked at their responses.

"How many of you plan to attend a Christian college or university after graduation?" Of the 76 Christian school graduates, five raised their hands.

"How many of you think God may be moving in your life toward some kind of ministry?" Of the 76 Christian school graduates, one raised his hand. One student out of 76 had been influenced toward ministry.

Perhaps my judgment is flawed, but it appears to me that some Christian school teachers didn't do their jobs.

But teachers might argue that their job is to teach math, or social studies or coach the basketball team. I disagree. Their job is to influence for God through teaching students, not subjects. If Christian school teachers teach only their subjects, even from a "Christian perspective," it's no wonder we're in the mess we're in. That's how we got where we are!

Education is for time and eternity. Christian school teachers who approach their vocation as educators for time alone would perhaps serve the Lord better in some other line of work. To have the opportunity to influence laborers to the whitened harvest fields and not use that influence has surely got to be a special kind of insensitivity to the Lord.

When I related my experience at the southern school graduation to a northern pastor whose church sponsors a Christian school, this pastor exclaimed wistfully, "In all the years we have had our Christian school, we have never had a student go off to college to train for the ministry."

Dear Christian school teacher, it is not necessary for you to spend your time competing with the public school system. Don't be a WAGAPS teacher, so preoccupied with professionalism that you have been diverted from the grand opportunity of kindly, lovingly, gently influencing those impressionable pupils toward eternal goals. After all, what you leave in your students' hearts is likely to be eternally more important than what you leave in their heads.

Christian education must never be permitted to be inferior. But the Christian teacher must never be a mere dispenser of information. He must be an influence for God. This influence is a sacred trust. The devil will do his best to divert us from it. In too many cases, he is incredibly successful.

– 8 –

The Abandoned Ministry Mission

How did we get where we are? How has the devil contributed to the ministry of the Word vanishing before our eyes? One of the more obvious though least admitted diversions of the devil is found in our colleges and universities. This diversion is obvious if viewed through the eye of history. It is far less obvious if viewed through the eye of current college literature.

One of the great allies to the vanishing ministry is the adaptation of education to the wants of the public rather than to its needs. With regard to education, this relates to colleges and universities broadening their curriculum to meet the vocational goals of society while at the same time minimally meeting the vocational goals of the church of Jesus Christ. Let me show you what I mean.

The training of the clergy has always held a prominent position in American education. In fact, more frequently than not it has occupied the premier position.

The first institution in American higher education, Harvard College, was founded in 1636 for the express purpose of training pastors. Until

1790 more than half of its graduates went directly into the ministry. An early booklet entitled "New England's First Fruits," distributed in England in 1643 to raise funds for the new college, stated the purpose of Harvard as that which led a student "to know God and Jesus Christ which is eternal life (John 17:3), and therefore to lay Christ in the bottom, as the only foundation of all sound knowledge and learning."[2]

The understanding during colonial days that the purpose of higher education was to train the clergy was so intense that scholars at Harvard believed the university man was in the "direct line of succession to the original prophets and apostles. The college was a local encampment of the universal 'militia' of Christ."[3]

The College of William and Mary was established in 1693 with "the avowed purpose of furnishing a seminary for ministers of the gospel. . . ."[4]

When Harvard became suspect of holding Unitarian and rationalistic views, Yale was founded in 1701 "to be a truer school of the prophets." In a pamphlet published in 1754, President Clap of Yale declared that "the great design of founding this school was to educate ministers in our own way." He went on to say that "colleges are societies of ministers, for training up persons for the work of the ministry." More conservative than Harvard from the start, until 1825 Yale sent an evangelistic team around the country proclaiming Jesus Christ as Saviour.

Rhode Island College, now known as Brown University, was founded by Baptists in 1764 for the primary task of training Baptist pastors. The purpose of Dartmouth College was similar. Though not founded to train pastors, it was initiated in 1769 to train men as missionaries to the American Indians.

The story continues the same. It is undeniable that pastoral training was the raison d'etre of higher education during the formative years of America. But with time things change.

Although pastoral training has historically worn the crown in American education, it has time and again been toppled from the throne. Note the following:

"While the majority of college graduates of the 17th century entered the ministry (as preachers or missionaries), this percentage dropped to 50% in 1750, 22% in 1801, and 6.5% in 1900. Among freshmen who entered college in the fall of 1980, less than half of 1% indicated 'clergy' as their probable career occupation."[5]

DECLINE IN CLERGY TRAINING IN AMERICAN EDUCATION

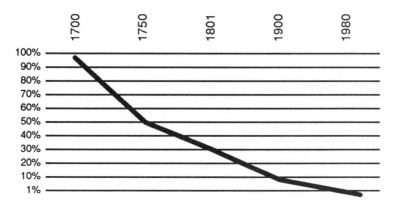

What are the factors in this downward spiral? As S. A. Witmer points out in his classic work, *Education With Dimension*, the declension in American higher education did not begin with liberalism but with loss in spiritual dynamic.[6] This was the result of a subtle change in mission. Increasingly colleges became aware that those not of the clergy needed to be educated as well. The narrowly defined purpose of education had to be broadened to accommodate this understanding. Thus, with the broadening of the mission came a corresponding declension in the number of pastoral candidates graduating from college.

There were other factors. Once the mission was changed, a change in emphasis soon followed. Institutions which once were church supported and controlled became publicly controlled. When public funds became the basis of college income, the ability to maintain private control was lost.

With a change in mission and a change in emphasis there was an honest and necessary change in curriculum. The educational needs of America demanded that courses in science, mathematics and related subjects be an integral part of the curriculum.

The broadening of the mission, the change in emphasis to include a wider population of students, and the change in curriculum to service this wider population all contributed to the fading strength of pastoral training in American education. Something had to be done.

Convinced that "learning is essential to preaching, but not the kind of learning required by university degrees,"[7] Charles Haddon Spurgeon established a pastor's college midway through the last century. Above all else Spurgeon wanted to train preachers and knew that "there is a learning that is essential to a successful ministry, viz. the learning of the whole Bible, to know God, by prayer, and experience of His dealings."[8]

H. Grattan Guinness founded The East London Institute for Home and Foreign Missions in 1872. Its purpose was to increase the number of missionaries. In the late 1800s, Albert B. Simpson returned from a visit to Great Britain where he had seen The East London Institute for Home and Foreign Missions in action. Simpson envisioned a school to train missionaries much as Spurgeon envisioned a school to train pastors. On October 1, 1883, the Missionary Training College for Home and Foreign Missions and Evangelists was organized (now Nyack College), and the Bible institute movement was born in America.

It wasn't long until the great American evangelist Dwight L. Moody called for the creation of a similar institution. Hence, the Bible Institute for Home and Foreign Missions, known after Moody's death as Moody Bible Institute, was born in 1886.

In 1900 several similar pastoral training schools were born. Practical Bible Training School, the institution I served as president for a decade, was among them. All had the same intent, i.e. to train pastors and missionaries because the public colleges and universities were not doing so anymore.

But, alas, even in this movement there has been an observable change in mission. This change is not recorded in college catalogs. You won't read of a change in promotional literature. But facts are facts.

In 1986 I was asked by the American Association of Bible Colleges to present a paper at their annual meeting in St. Paul, Minnesota. The paper was entitled, "The State of Pastoral Training in America." In preparation for this presentation I questioned one hundred Christian seminaries, universities, colleges and Bible colleges in America with regard to the number of pastoral majors graduating in the class of 1986. The results of this survey were not heartening. They are printed in full in Appendix A.

Briefly what I learned was this. Whereas most Christian institutions in America today continue with the same written purpose with which they were founded, the de facto purpose has changed dramatically.

Those students graduating from Christian seminaries in the Class of 1986 who intended to enter the pastorate accounted for 48 percent of the total graduating class. Although this percentage is almost half, one might have thought it would be almost whole. The percentage of students in Bible colleges who graduated in 1986 intending to enter the pastorate was 29 percent. In the Christian university or Christian graduate school the number was 8 percent. And in the Christian liberal arts college, only 5 percent of the total graduating class of 1986 intended to enter the pastorate.

Certainly this does not necessarily mean that the other students in these institutions were out of or evading the will of God. That's not the point. The point is that when the Harvards and Yales abandoned the mission of training men and women for ministry, the Christian seminary and Christian college arose to fill the gap. And now there appears to be a de facto abandonment of that same mission in these circles.

Again, the stated purpose of most of our Christian institutions of higher education still focuses on training for ministry, but the number of pastors and missionaries graduated from some of these institutions could hold their alumni meetings in a phone booth.

Although we would never expect 100 percent of any of these institutions' graduates to be heading out for the mission field, where should we look for the candidates needed to fill God's vineyard? Where are the institutions whose mission has not been broadened so that business and elementary education have supplanted the pastoral major as the largest major in the institution? Who really is placing the emphasis on training pastors and missionaries? We know which institutions claim to be doing this, for we have read their promotional literature. But a quick look at the majors on a graduation program jolts us back to reality.

All Satan must do to reduce effective training for lifetime ministry is to make other legitimate majors grow and flourish in our colleges and seminaries while the pastoral and missions majors languish. That is the case presently in many of our fine institutions.

Our best and brightest candidates for lifetime service to the Lord are being siphoned into other legitimate careers while many theological and Bible institutions appear to be drifting from their original purpose. They have broadened their mission and their curriculum to meet society's needs, but in so doing have significantly reduced the number of men and women meeting the church's needs.

Christian seminary and college trustees and administrators are well advised to look carefully at their products. Are the majority of your graduates entering careers that square with the stated mission of your institution? Are the majority of them leaving the hallowed halls of your institution to serve mankind or the Master? Or, are you further along the path of those Harvards and Yales that have preceded you than you care to admit? Are you couching secular education in sacred rhetoric?

These are not easy questions for Christian institutions to ask of themselves. They are even more difficult to answer honestly. But the path of American higher education is very clear, and the similarities in progression down that path of many of our former and present Christian institutions are striking. Too striking!

The devil's diversion cuts across every level of the Christian spectrum, but nowhere does it cut more deeply than here.

– 9 –

The Blitzkrieg Call

Pilots of the German Luftwaffe during the Second World War used a tactic of swift and pinpoint flying to establish what has become known as lightning warfare — Blitzkrieg. Since that time the word "blitzkrieg" has come to describe anything that happens quickly and dramatically. Some people look for the call of God on their lives to come in this manner.

In Acts 9, Saul of Tarsus was traveling to Damascus to place in chains any people he found who had received Christ as Saviour. As he journeyed, it happened. The blitzkrieg call. "Suddenly there shined round about him a light from heaven: and he fell to the earth, and heard a voice saying unto him, Saul, Saul, why persecutest thou me?" (Acts 9:3-4).

What a tremendous experience this was for Paul. He never got over it. It was the call of God upon his life in an unforgettable way. It would be hard to deny this call; it would be impossible to walk away from it.

I suppose if everyone received the call to lifetime ministry this same way, the blitzkrieg method, we would be more sure who had it and who did not. Unfortunately, the call doesn't always come this way. In fact, it rarely ever comes this way. Still, the devil has diverted more than a few young people from lifetime service to the Lord simply by convincing them that since they experienced no blitzkrieg call, they experienced no call at all. That's how we got where we are in the vanishing ministry.

Consider another example from the Book of Acts. This is more the normative call of God. There were no flashes of light, no rumblings of thunder, no bells, no voices, just the quiet confirmation of God's call.

Apparently the Apostle Paul had the joy of leading Timothy to the Lord on his first missionary journey to Asia minor. He undertook that journey with his sidekick and apostolic equal, Barnabas. But when the two men planned a second missionary journey, there was sharp contention between them about taking young John Mark with them again. So firm was each man in his opinion that they decided to go their separate ways rather than allow the dispute to disrupt the cause of Christ.

When Paul set out alone on the second journey, he was clearly looking for a partner. Let's allow the text to speak for itself. "Then came he to Derbe and Lystra: and, behold, a certain disciple was there, named Timotheus, the son of a certain woman, which was a Jewess, and believed; but his father was a Greek: which was well reported of by the brethren that were at Lystra and Iconium. Him would Paul have to go forth with him" (Acts 16:1-3).

Timothy had been in the community of faith long enough to grow in grace and in the knowledge of our Lord and Saviour Jesus Christ. He had developed rapidly though steadily as a believer. The elders in Lystra and Iconium had watched his progress with thanksgiving. He was well reported of by these godly men.

What is striking here is that there is no mention of God's call on Timothy's life. I don't doubt that there was such a call, but it was apparently so commonplace that it did not deserve mention in the narrative. The godly elders recognized Timothy's gifts, commended him to the apostle, and Paul simply said, "I want you!" There was no discussion. There were no voices, no inner revelations, just quiet obedience to the will of God.

How spectacular do you think the call of God was on our Lord's disciples? Read the accounts in the Gospels; it's pretty tame stuff. Matthew 4:18 records that Jesus was simply walking by the Sea of

Galilee, saw Peter and Andrew, and said unto them, "Follow me, and I will make you fishers of men." Matthew records, "And they straightway left their nets, and followed him" (Matt. 4:20). The call of James and John was almost identical.

Matthew's own call to lifetime service was not much to write home about either. He records it this way: "And as Jesus passed forth from thence, he saw a man, named Matthew, sitting at the receipt of custom: and he saith unto him, Follow me. And he arose, and followed him" (Matt. 9:9).

Philip's call was equally unspectacular. It is matter-of-factly mentioned in John 1:43: "The day following Jesus would go forth into Galilee, and findeth Philip, and saith unto him, Follow me."

The call of the other disciples isn't even recorded in detail.

So, if budding preachers and missionaries are looking for burning bushes, fireflashes from heaven or angelic announcements, they can forget it. God doesn't normally work that way. He works quietly — convicting, convincing and confirming that He has a work for us to do.

How then can you determine whether or not you are called of God to lifetime ministry? You must ask questions, especially three specific and simple questions. Here they are.

First, ask yourself, "Am I called to serve the Lord?" If you are saved, you are called to serve the Lord. Let's establish that at the start. Every born-again man, woman or child is called to serve the Lord. That is the purpose of our salvation.

It's a shame to quote Ephesians 2:8-9 without quoting verse 10. Verses 8 and 9 tell us how we are saved; verse 10 tells us why. "For we are his workmanship, created in Christ Jesus unto good works, which God hath before ordained that we should walk in them."

Are you called to serve the Lord? If you're alive and a Christian, you're called to serve the Lord. We are not saved to sit, soak and sour; we are saved to serve.

The second question is this: "How am I called to serve the Lord?" This is where the specificity of God's call enters the picture. If you are a believer and therefore are called to serve the Lord, how will you do it? Romans 12 provides the answer.

After those two initial and very important "living sacrifice" verses Paul says, "For as we have many members in one body, and all members have not the same office: So we, being many, are one body in Christ, and every one members one of another. Having then gifts differing according to the grace that is given to us . . ." (Rom. 12:4-6).

How are you to serve the Lord? As God has gifted you, that's how. There is no call to ministry that is not first a call to Christ, but once we have recognized that all believers are called to serve the Lord, the question of how is determined by our gifts. God gifts His children for particular service, and if a pastor sees a young man in his church who is gifted for ministry, what right does that pastor have to send him off to the state university to major in computer science? He has no right at all!

I believe fully that God does not call us to a specific ministry and not gift us for that ministry. But conversely, I believe just as strongly that God does not gift us for a specific ministry and not call us to it. "For the gifts and calling of God are without repentance." God doesn't waste His gifts.

Does this mean there is no definite call of God on a person's life? Not at all! The call of God is specific; it is supernatural. But, it is rarely sudden; it is rarely spectacular. The call of God most frequently comes to a yielded and tender spirit and is spiritually discerned, not spectacularly displayed.

This leaves the third question. If you are called to serve the Lord and your gifts tell you how you are to serve Him, the only question left is, "Where do I serve the Lord?" This is the most difficult question of all. Again we must rely on the gentle leading of the Holy Spirit.

The Spirit of God does not work in a vacuum, and it is at this point that serious servants gather all the material they can about the needs of the world and how their spiritual gifts can meet those needs. Serious servants who need training in the Word gather all the catalogs they can of institutions which have a strong program in Bible and ministry skills. Serious servants do not choose a college curriculum that will teach them how to serve mankind only. Serious servants choose a college curriculum that will teach them how to save mankind, through the grace of God.

The devil has been incredibly successful in diverting men and women from lifetime service to the Lord just by confusing them about the call to service. I have always heard that if a man can do anything other than preach he should never aspire to preach the Word. Although I understand this thinking, it does not appear to me that we have great numbers of men in evangelical pulpits today who do not belong there.

But it does appear that we have great numbers of men in evangelical congregations today who belong in pulpits. Are not the laborers few? Does that mean God has incorrectly calculated how many pastors and missionaries He needs? I don't think so.

There is certainly nothing wrong in being a plumber, a pipefitter or a postman. This world needs all of these, and you can enjoy any of these occupations and still use your gifts for God. But if you feel you are gifted to preach the Word, if you see the desperate need for preachers, and if you feel that gentle tug from the Holy Spirit to exercise your gifts in a way that better serves eternity, what are you waiting for? Throw down that plunger, that pipe, that Publisher's Clearing House envelope and pick up the powerful and living Word of God.

If the blitzkrieg call were necessary for ministry, most of us would be in another line of work today. It isn't necessary. In fact, it isn't characteristic of the way God works in the lives of men and women to convince them of lifetime service. Listen to His gentle prodding, hear His still small voice, examine your gifts, and assume He wants you in lifetime ministry. When you step out in faith, He will confirm His call. You'll know.

– 10 –

Eli Syndrome Pastors

I grew up in a pastor's home. I know pastors are busy people. I have pastored myself. I know pastors are busy people. I have preached in over 100 churches a year for years. I know pastors are busy people, but some pastors are both busy and productive; others are just busy.

Because there are more demands on a pastor's day than hours to fulfill them, the busy pastor must be certain that the most important things are getting done while other things are delegated to subordinates. Delegation is a useful tool of leadership, but pastors must never delegate what God has specifically designed for and demanded of them.

One of those designs is for the pastor to be a mentor, to take under his wing young fledglings with potential for ministry. There is frequent evidence of this role in Scripture, but when a pastor abdicates this role, it leads to a vanishing ministry. That's how we got where we are.

Moses was a mighty man of God. In fact, so mighty was he that Deuteronomy 34:10 testifies, "There arose not a prophet since in Israel like unto Moses, whom the LORD knew face to face." He delivered God's people from centuries of cruel Egyptian bondage. Moses would be a tough act to follow.

Still, the Book of Joshua begins with the matter-of-fact statement, "Now after the death of Moses the servant of the LORD it came to pass, that the LORD spake unto Joshua the son of Nun, Moses' minister" (Joshua 1:1). God promised the fledgling understudy, "As I was with Moses, so I will be with thee" (Joshua 1:5).

Elijah was a flaming prophet of God. A strange looking and volatile man, his last flamboyant act was to wrap his mantle together, smite the waters of the Jordan River so that Elisha, his understudy, and he could cross over on dry ground (2 Kings 2:8). Then he disappeared in a chariot of fire into heaven. Elijah would be a tough act to follow.

Still, no sooner had Elijah gone in a flash than Elisha took that same mantle which Elijah left behind and smote those same waters of the Jordan River so that they again parted and he could return to Canaan on dry land.

There was really no one in the early church to rival the Apostle Paul. He was a scholar, a church planter, a teacher, a preacher, an author and much more. He was such a commanding figure that he even withstood the fiery Peter to the face. He would be a tough act to follow.

Still, when Paul was in prison in Rome for the last time and writing his final letter to Timothy, his own son in the faith, he lamented, "At my first answer no man stood with me, but all men forsook me" (2 Tim. 4:16). And of Timothy, his fledgling understudy, Paul once said, "I have no man likeminded" (Phil. 2:20).

Moses was busy with the murmuring millions. Elijah was busy with the prophets of Baal. Paul was busy with the care of the churches. But all of them had one thing in common. While they were busy doing those things which would make them tough acts to follow, they had enough time to disciple those who would follow them. They were sensitive to the call of God on the lives of their understudies.

Eli the priest, on the other hand, is a different story. Oh yes, he had a fledgling understudy, the boy Samuel, just like Moses, Elijah and Paul. But he had little time to be a mentor to his understudy. He was too busy with the routine of the ministry.

Eli was so busy with the work at Shiloh, so involved with the details of ministry, he forgot the people around him. He never chastened his sons, and they disgraced him. He lived a faithless life before Jehovah, and He cursed him. But equally tragic was Eli's flawed relationship to Samuel. First Samuel 3 tells the story all too graphically.

The word of the Lord was sparse in those days. The prophets were not hearing from God as they once did. Every word from God was like a precious drop of moisture on a parched tongue. This condition makes the fact that God spoke three times to young Samuel all the more astounding.

Three times in the middle of the night God came to Eli's understudy and called his name. Three times the young man responded to God. Three times he went to his mentor for advice. You know the story.

Eli told Samuel the first time, "Go back to bed!" Samuel soon returned, and again the old priest was insensitive to God's call on his understudy, telling him to go back to bed. Samuel returned, and it was only on the third occasion that Eli discerned it was God's call his fledgling was hearing.

Eli had a problem with inattention to the voice of God. When the boy received God's call, the priest of God, who ought to have recognized it, didn't.

I fear that growing numbers of pastors today are so weighed down with the details and problems of the ministry that they have lost meaningful contact with the people around them. Most pastors today do not have a mentor relationship like Moses to Joshua, Elijah to Elisha, or Paul to Timothy. Most do not have young Samuels whom they are regularly discipling. Others may know who their understudies should be but are inattentive to the call of God on their young Samuels.

Some time ago I was asked by a group of pastors whom I admire deeply to present the findings of my survey of pastoral training in America. After the presentation there was time for questions and answers. I asked, "How many of you pastors, if you came up through the church, can identify what it was your pastor did to influence you toward ministry?" Of the 40 or so pastors present almost all hands went up immediately. "My pastor had me lead the singing." "My pastor used to take all of us young people to the county nursing home each Sunday afternoon for a service." "My pastor took us to youth conferences every year."

The answers were all different; yet, they were all the same. Their pastor got them involved in ministry. He had them up and doing things in the church every time the doors were open. One week they would read the Scripture; the next week they may take up the offering. But they knew that there always would be something.

After this rapid fire exchange I asked these pastors another question.

"Pastor, what are you doing today in your church to involve your young people the way your pastor involved you?" No hands immediately went up. The silence was deafening. The conclusion was evident. Many pastors are contributing to the vanishing ministry just because they are insensitive to the need to involve their young people in ministry and help them hear God's voice.

Pastor, when was the last time a young person in your congregation came to you and said they thought God was speaking to them about lifetime service to the Lord? Did you say something like, "Oh, that's nice," the 20th-century equivalent of Eli's "Go back to bed"?

Now more than ever pastors need to have attentive ears when God speaks to their fledglings. We must listen with them. Frequently we must listen for them. We must keep an eagle eye on our congregations and consistently single out those best qualified for service to the Lord. We must develop a mentor relationship with them. We must do all we can to involve them in meaningful ministry and to aid them in hearing God's call on their life.

Paul's admonition to his Timothy was, "Thou therefore, my son, be strong in the grace that is in Christ Jesus. And the things that thou hast heard of me among many witnesses, the same commit thou to faithful men, who shall be able to teach others also" (2 Tim. 2:1-2).

Would the apostle's admonition be any less to us if we were his Timothy? Should we not find some faithful men and commit to them what we have learned so that they can commit these things to other faithful men? Should we not be on the constant lookout for these faithful young men and young women?

If the devil can get the pastor to snooze on into the Eli syndrome, if he can get the pastor so bogged down with details he has little time for people, if that subtle snake can get the pastor insensitive to the call of God on those around him, he will have destroyed not only an understudy but a mentor as well.

How did we get where we are? How did the devil accomplish a declining enrollment of young men and women for lifetime ministry? Diversion. If he can divert the pastor, he can divert anyone.

Conclusion

We have met the enemy and it is us. While doing other things, good things, necessary things, the pastor, the Christian school teacher, the parent has forfeited a grand opportunity to recruit a young man or young woman for lifetime ministry. While being in the world but not of it, we have become so comfortable in it that our goals and purposes in life are not discernibly different from unsaved people around us.

That which is of eternal importance has been forced to take a back seat to that which is of temporal convenience. We have become more and more interested in working for these 70 years we live on this earth. Does that mean we have become less and less interested in working for the endless ages of eternity? In some cases, I'm afraid it does.

Again and again Satan has diverted God's army. Again and again he has confused us about our responsibility to the Commander-in-Chief. Again and again he has vividly shown us the legitimate needs of this world to which we could dedicate our lives. Again and again Satan has plotted for what is good to rob us of what is best.

We did not get to this low point in the battle deliberately. And we did not get here with our eyes wide open. Satan worked subtly to get our eyes off the Commander and onto ourselves. We were duped; all of us were tricked. But now we know it. Maybe we could claim innocence before when the ranks of God's soldiers were rapidly depleting, but what will we claim in the future?

If you have asked God henceforth to keep Satan's devilish diversion from you, watch out! That will call for some heart-searching decisions and will undoubtedly affect every area of your life. Are you ready for that?

Part Three

The Company of the Committed

What attitudes are needed for ministry?

The Company of the Committed

What attitudes are needed for ministry?

It's time we looked inward. Is there within me the right stuff to make a good soldier for Christ? Do I have the right attitude about serving the Lord? What attitudes are necessary if more young and old alike are to answer the call to lifetime ministry?

Although more attitudes than these are necessary to make a good harvester in God's field, the following attitudes seem to be the ones in the most glaring absence today. The recovery of these attitudes by Christians sensitive to the Lord will be necessary if the vanishing ministry is to cease vanishing. What are these important attitudes?

– 11 –

The Attitude of Commitment

There is an amazing lack of commitment in our society today. The collapse of commitment is seen everywhere. Workers in the Western world show an appalling lack of productivity because they show an appalling lack of commitment toward the products they produce.

Such lack of commitment is perhaps most graphically seen in marriages. In order to accommodate this declining commitment, pre-nuptial agreements have become popular in which both parties agree on divorce settlements before they tie the knot. Some have changed the marriage vows to read, "For as long as you both shall love." Remember when it was "For as long as you both shall live"? And not long ago a sign appeared in the window of New York City jewelry store which read, "Wedding Rings for rent." It was bound to happen.

This lack of commitment easily spills over into the Christian world. Pastoral tenure at churches is becoming alarmingly short. Christian colleges once committed to pastoral and missionary training are now cranking out businessmen, teachers and scientists by the score, but hardly any preachers.

What is commitment anyway? I define the term as the quality of tenaciously pursuing to the very end, with heart and soul, what we have pledged to pursue.

There is a delightfully committed person tucked away in the pages of the New Testament. He is a good example of one who tenaciously pursued to the very end, with heart and soul, what he pledged to pursue. His name is Onesiphorus.

In his last epistle Paul refers to Onesiphorus twice. These are the only two places he is mentioned in the Bible. He commends this little-known saint for being committed to him and in so doing points out the three qualities necessary in true commitment. They are consistency, initiative and determination.

In 2 Timothy 1:16 the apostle says of Onesiphorus, "He oft refreshed me." Two verses later Paul declares, "In how many things he ministered unto me at Ephesus, thou knowest very well." That's the consistency of commitment.

Commitment was not a once-in-awhile thing with Onesiphorus; it was an all-the-time thing. Paul could count on him. We are not aware how often he refreshed the apostle or even what this means. But Paul wants us to know that Onesiphorus was consistent in his refreshment.

The attitude of commitment, the ability to be counted on, is frequently non-existent in many Christians today. Not so with Onesiphorus, and not so with Daniel Conn.

For 40 years Daniel Conn was the grounds keeper on the campus at the Bible college I served as president. He is now with the Lord, but for those 40 years Mr. Conn was always there, repairing boilers, planting flowers, raking leaves, whatever it took. In the last summer of his life he planted 3,300 marigolds on the campus, plus other flowers.

One night I was awakened at 3:00 a.m. in my campus home by the sound of running water. I bounded out of bed to see if a faucet was leaking in the kitchen or bathroom. None was. I could still hear water running. After an unsuccessful search all through the house, I heard a noise outside. Going to the window, I saw Mr. Conn watering the flowers, tulips as I remember.

I said to him, "What's the matter? Can't you sleep?"

"Sure I can sleep," he responded, "but this is the best time to water these flowers." He was watering the flowers at 3:00 a.m. Initially I thought he was crazy, but that's not crazy; that's commitment.

What caused Daniel Conn to water flowers when others forgot? Consistency. You could count on him. He would always be there. He would consistently do whatever it took to get the job done, regardless of the cost to him. Onesiphorus was like that.

Another quality of commitment demonstrated by Onesiphorus is initiative. In 2 Timothy 1:17 Paul notes, "But, when he was in Rome, he sought me out . . ." Paul did not call for Onesiphorus to come to him. Onesiphorus took the initiative to go to Paul, for Paul needed refreshing.

Commitment always starts with the subject, not the object. If the object is worthy, if the cause is worthy, if the person is worthy, the object, cause or person will still be worthy whether or not we are committed to it. Commitment does not begin with the object. Commitment begins when we pledge ourselves to that worthy person or object.

Was not Paul worthy of refreshment by others? Of course he was. Why, then, was Onesiphorus the only one who often refreshed him? Because of the initiative of commitment. Onesiphorus initiated the commitment when he pledged to himself that regardless of the cost he would refresh the apostle.

A final quality of Onesiphorus' commitment toward Paul is the determination of that commitment. Again notice 2 Timothy 1:17. "He sought me out, very diligently." Onesiphorus had the grit and guts to stick it out.

It would have been frightfully easy for Onesiphorus to return to Ephesus and report to the church there that although he had attempted to locate the apostle and refresh him, he was unsuccessful in doing so. After all, Rome was a big city. It would not be easy to find Paul. Not easy, that is, except for one thing — the determination of commitment.

Isaiah said, "The Lord God will help me; therefore shall I not be confounded: therefore have I set my face like a flint; I know that I shall not be ashamed" (Isa. 50:7). That's determination!

Of Jesus it was said, "Who for the joy that was set before him endured the cross, despising the shame" (Heb. 12:2). That's determination!

Paul was counseled not to go to Jerusalem, and he replied, "What mean ye to weep and to break mine heart? For I am ready not to be bound only, but also to die at Jerusalem for the name of the Lord Jesus" (Acts 21:13). That's commitment!

Commitment demands the determination to remain committed, regardless of the circumstances. Onesiphorus had such commitment.

That's why the next three little words in 2 Timothy 1:17 are so very important — "and found me."

Onesiphorus was determined to find Paul and refresh him. Nothing would stand in his way. He knew that the purpose of commitment is not to run the race but to win it. He wasn't in Rome to give locating Paul the old college try. He wasn't there to try at all. He was there to succeed in locating Paul.

We need lifetime servants in the harvest fields at this very moment. But the kind of servants needed are not the kind who give it their best shot. The kind of servants needed are those who will tenaciously pursue to the very end, with heart and soul, what they have pledged to pursue.

In the secular world 33 percent of all overseas employees return to the USA within the first year. It's tough out there, and perhaps this is why it has been calculated that up to half of all new missionaries do not last beyond their first term on the field.[1] The typical length of service in the decade of the '80s is between two and ten years on the field.

The missionary enterprise cannot afford to recruit potential missionaries who are not going to make it past the first term of service. The church of Jesus Christ needs men like Onesiphorus, not men like Demas (see 2 Timothy 4:10). Lifetime service means just that — lifetime service, a commitment to serve the Lord with consistence, with initiative, with determination never to quit.

Paul said, "Know ye not that they which run in a race run all, but one receiveth the prize? So run, that ye may obtain" (1 Cor. 9:24). Paul appreciated helpers like Onesiphorus because he tenaciously pursued to the very end, with heart and soul, what he had pledged to pursue.

Onesiphorus was interested in only one thing— success in completing the task he had pledged to complete. That's the kind of attitude that makes a lifetime servant. After all, when we meet our Master in heaven, do we really think He will alter His promised blessing and say, "Well tried, thou good and faithful servant . . ." (Matt. 25:21)?

The attitude of commitment. Don't leave home without it!

– 12 –

The Attitude of Compassion

Recently in a large city a rather unique marathon was run. It was unique because the streets were not cleared for the runners. Fans and well-wishers did not line the streets; but instead, they crowded them, making the runner's task that much more difficult. Also, each runner was required to carry with him any water or nourishment he would need for the entire race. No one along the route could hand a cool drink to the runner. Most of the runners chose to take just a small amount of water, and some even took a granola bar or two with them for energy.

Among the runners in this unique race were three friends. We'll call them Demas, Mark and Timothy (not their real names). Each of them approached the marathon a bit differently.

Demas took a small amount of water and only one granola bar. "Just enough to get me through," was his reasoning. Mark took two bottles of water and about half-a-dozen granola bars. He was prepared for just about anything. Then there was Tim. He had nearly a dozen bottles of water and twice that many granola bars. "You've got enough there to feed the whole field of runners and most of the onlookers," laughed Demas. Mark agreed.

Well, the race began. All three friends were off like a shot, setting a pretty fast pace. During the course of the race many runners passed them by, and still others lagged behind them. After about 20 minutes Tim began to tire.

He's the one who was loaded down with granola bars. Demas sarcastically chided Tim, "Get rid of all that junk or you'll never finish the race." But Tim continued. Soon Mark began to tire as well, even though he had half the burden Tim had. "You're as bad as Tim," laughed Demas. "You ought to run more like me."

As they wound their way through the streets of the city, the field began to thin out. One by one runners were dropping out of the race.

One section of the course took the runners through a rather depressed area of the city. People came out of their rundown houses to see the runners pass by. These were people in desperate need, and watching the race was one of the few pleasures of life for them.

When Demas got to this section of the course, he just whizzed by the onlookers. By this time he was far ahead of his friends. Mark eventually arrived at the same section of town and decided to throw a couple of granola bars to those standing by. After all, they looked as if they could use them, and the bars were just slowing him down anyway.

After a long while Tim passed the same point. By this time he was exhausted. His heavy burden had gotten to him. He knew he had to do something about it or he would never finish the race. The water and granola bars had to go!

As Tim slowed to a snail's pace, he could peer into the faces of the onlookers. He began to distribute his bottles of water and the granola bars to eagerly outstretched hands. It became evident. They had a need, and he had a burden. He would have to stop and discharge his burden entirely if he wanted to be successful.

And then a very strange thing happened. Tim discovered he was compassionate toward the onlookers and found that unloading his burden and meeting their needs became more important to him than

winning the race. Suddenly the meaning of the race took on a whole new dimension.

At the end of the course Demas crossed the finish line in a new personal best time for him. He was traveling lightly and was able to cruise to the finish line unaffected by the surroundings through which he ran. About half-an-hour later Mark crossed the finish line into the waiting arms of his friend. "What took you so long?" Demas questioned. "You were right," Mark managed to say. "I carried too much of a burden to accomplish my personal goals. I'll never do that again!"

And what about Tim? Where was he? Weighed down by his burden, he was far behind doing something about the load he carried and finding new meaning to life in the process. In fact, Tim was winning the race, and he didn't even realize it.

By now you have guessed that this strange race never actually took place. It is a parable. In fact, although it never happened in the real world, it happens daily in the spiritual world.

Demas represents those Christians who are in the heavenly race but care little about those who are not. They are of no concern to him, and thus he carried no burden for them, only for himself.

Mark represents those Christians who are in the heavenly race and do care about those who are not. These Christians have granola and water to give. If you will, they have the Bread and Water of Life and are somewhat interested in sharing what they have with those in need. They ease their burden when they share their provision.

And Timothy represents those Christians who are in the heavenly race and care deeply about those who are not. These Christians are heavily burdened. Their burden will keep them from winning the praise of men, but it will win for them the praise of God.

The vanishing ministry will never stop vanishing as long as the ranks of the runners are filled with the Demases of this world. Christians who have little or no burden for the lost are not attuned to the heart of God and will never hear the call of God.

In fact, we will continue to lose the war against Satan if we have only Marks as runners. A little burden is a dangerous thing. It isn't so heavy that we have to stop and do something about it. In fact, many Christians have resigned themselves to carrying a little burden for the lost right to the end of life's race. We throw crumbs here and there along the way, but the passersby need whole loaves of bread. People like Mark will keep us in the race, but we will never win it.

In this parable, the attitude of compassion for the lost is best exhibited by Tim. He realizes he must do something about his burden for the lost; otherwise he will finish the race but lose the reason for running it. The passersby will all die in their sins.

The Gospels are filled with examples of Jesus' compassion for those around Him. He had compassion for two blind men (Matt. 20:34); for the leper who needed to be cleansed (Mark 1:41); for the demon-possessed man (Mark 5:19); for the 5,000 who needed to be fed (Mark 6:34); for the 4,000 who needed to be fed (Mark 8:2); for the boy with the dumb spirit (Mark 9:22); and for the widow of Nain (Luke 7:13). Each of these verses makes reference to our Lord's compassion on the physical needs of people. Read them!

But His greater burden, His greater compassion, was for their spiritual needs. When He approached the city of Jerusalem from the Mount of Olives, "he beheld the city, and wept over it," discerning the spiritual blindness of the Jews. It's that attitude of compassion that creates a burden for the lost.

We are quite familiar with our Lord's teaching to the disciples, "The harvest truly is plenteous, but the laborers are few" (Matt. 9:37). We may not be as familiar, however, at what prompted Him to say this. The preceding verse says, "But when he saw the multitudes, he was moved with compassion on them, because they fainted, and were scattered abroad, as sheep having no shepherd." It was Christ's compassion on the multitudes that initiated His call for more laborers.

And there can be little question that the Father's burden for a sinful race stemmed from His compassion for us as people. The most important verse in the Bible is still, "For God so loved the world, that he gave his only begotten Son, that whosoever believeth in him should not perish, but have everlasting life" (John 3:16). The plan to save came from the burden for the unsaved, which in turn found its derivation in God's love for the world.

Rich compassion creates a rich burden, and a rich burden cannot be borne; it must be cared for. The greater the attitude of compassion for the lost is among Christians, the greater the burden for the lost. Like Timothy, we will not be able simply to run in life's race anymore with such a burden; we will be compelled to act on it.

A prime example of this in the Bible is found in Acts 17. Here is recorded the plight of Paul. He had preached in the synagogue of Thessalonica until he was ejected from that synagogue. The whole city was in an uproar, and Paul and Silas had to flee by night to Berea. Undaunted, Paul began to preach in the Berean synagogue until some Jews of Thessalonica came to Berea and stirred up trouble again. Hence, Silas and Timothy remained at Berea with the fledgling church while Paul was conducted south to Athens.

Paul had been through two harrowing experiences in a short period of time. When he arrived in Athens, no one would have criticized him for taking a little "R and R" in the Athens Hilton. After all, he deserved it. While he waited for a report from Silas and Timothy, he easily could have rested and relaxed. But not Paul!

Acts 17:16 records, "Now while Paul waited for them at Athens, his spirit was stirred in him, when he saw the city wholly given to idolatry." It was just too much for Paul. Here was a city without Christ, wholly given to idolatry. How could he be still? His spirit was stirred within him.

That is the spirit of compassion. It generated a burden for the Athenians which caused Paul to leave the comfort and safety of his room, to dispute with the Jews in the synagogue until he was thrown out of it, and then to continue the disputation with them in the marketplace daily. The attitude of compassion made him weep in his heart for the brilliant Athenians, and that compassion became the ground for a genuine burden for the lost.

The ministry wanes and ultimately vanishes when the burden for lost souls wanes and ultimately disappears. That burden is not something that can be trumped up. It is not something that can be ignored. And it certainly is not something that can be carried throughout life, if it is a large enough burden.

Robert Murray McCheyne was one of the most powerful preachers of the gospel to grace this earth. He preached his heart out in Dundee, Scotland, before the Lord took him home at the early age of 29. Once a preacher visited McCheyne's church in Dundee and stood in the pulpit before an empty sanctuary. Unknown to him, the sexton of the church was in the back cleaning. The sexton interrupted the silence by asking, "Do you want to preach like McCheyne?"

Startled, the preacher replied, "Yes."

"Then come with me," said the sexton. He took the preacher into McCheyne's study where everything was essentially just as McCheyne had left it.

"Now sit in the chair," ordered the sexton. The preacher rounded the corner of the pastor's desk and sat down. "Now put your elbows on the desk." The preacher complied. "Now cup your hands and bury your face in your hands." Once again the guest complied.

"Now let the tears flow," said the discerning old sexton. "That's how McCheyne did it!"

Little will be accomplished in ministry without a genuine burden for the lost. This is a major ingredient in being a lifetime servant of the Lord. "He that goeth forth and weepeth, bearing precious seed, shall doubtless come again with rejoicing, bringing his sheaves with him" (Psalm 126:6). Compassion.

Request it and respond to it. Ask and act!

– 13 –

The Attitude of Pliability

A *most important* attitude for anyone who would yield to lifetime service for the Lord is pliability. This is the ability to be molded, to be pressured, to be fashioned into whatever God wants us to be, and to be so with a right attitude about it.

The figure of the potter and the clay occurs again and again in the Bible, and with very good reason. While watching a potter we learn lessons that cannot be learned as well by any other figure. We want to learn lessons about the attitude of pliability as it relates to the vanishing ministry.

The teaching of God's Word about the potter and his clay can be summarized in five great truths. They are these.

God Is the Potter; We Are the Clay.

Sounds simple enough, doesn't it? Still, the point of this truth is frequently missed, perhaps due to its simplicity.

The Old Testament prophet Isaiah said it this way. "But now, O LORD, thou art our father; we are the clay, and thou our potter; and we all are the work of thy hand" (Isa. 64:8). Since God is the Potter and we are the clay, we have some sort of relationship with Him. It's a relationship not to be sniffed at.

The Potter is also our Father. That gives Him a family relationship to us. We are not just a lump of clay; we are His kith and kin. We are, and I mean this reverently, a "chip off the old block." The Potter takes special care with His clay, for it is His children.

Also, did you notice that Isaiah said of God, "thou (art) our potter"? That gives us a personal relationship to Him. The Sovereign God of the universe, the Creator of all things, is our personal Potter. That gives me a good feeling about my future.

And then, too, the prophet said, "We are all the work of thy hand." My Father is the Potter. He is my personal Potter. And I receive personal attention from my Potter. I am not a product of evolutionary development or angelic mass production, but I am handmade, handcrafted by the most skilled Craftsman imaginable (cf. Job 10:8; Psalm 119:73).

Be that as it may, we must still remember who is who. He is the Potter; we are the clay. That means He does the forming, the plying, the shaping. We are the ones formed, plied and shaped. He calls the shots, not us. He is Almighty God; He is our Heavenly Father; He is our loving Potter. If we understand this relationship correctly, we won't have any problems getting along with God.

The Potter Molds the Clay as He Wills

The second great truth in the potter's relationship to the clay is that the potter is absolutely sovereign over the clay. He does with the clay whatever pleases him, and he doesn't consult the clay about it. The same is true about God, our Potter.

In teaching the Christians of ancient Rome about God's absolute sovereignty Paul asks the question, "Hath not the potter power over the clay, of the same lump to make one vessel unto honor, and another unto dishonor?" (Rom. 9:21). The implied answer is, "Yes!" The potter has absolute power over the clay, to make of it any vessel he wants.

I had the delightful opportunity to take my last semester in seminary at the University of Strasbourg in the Alsatian region of France. I loved it. And since I had my weekends free, I decided to take in some of the French and Alsatian culture while I lived there. A favorite weekend hangout of mine was the tiny town of Oberbetschdorf, north of Strasbourg. This town was a potter's town. It seemed that everyone in the town was a potter by trade.

The townspeople were friendly and would invite you into their homes to watch them ply their trade. I was fascinated. The potters would take a lump of clay, about ten inches square, place it on their wheel, and with their feet begin the spinning of the wheel. Then from a water hose, extending down from the ceiling above them, they would draw water and begin to work with that lump of clay as the wheel whizzed around.

To me the most incredible thing was the control the potter had over the clay. Once he moistened the clay and thus softened it, he was absolute master of the clay. With boyish wonder I would say to the potter, "Make a tall thin vase out of the clay," and quick as a wink the lump was two feet tall. Then I'd say, "Now make a short fat pot out of it." Just as quickly it was only six inches tall but two feet in diameter. I was impressed. That potter did with clay exactly as he pleased.

So it is with the Christian when he or she is moistened with the water of the Word and softened by the Spirit of God. Our Father, the Potter, does with us whatever He pleases. He molds us as He wills. If He wishes to mold us into a lifetime servant, we are ready.

The Clay Must Not Question the Potter's Plan

Here's a third truth about the potter and his clay. When the potter sits at his wheel, he has a mental image of what he ultimately wants the lump of clay to look like. This mental plan is not revealed to the clay beforehand, or even afterward. The potter proceeds according to that plan. It's his plan, not the clay's plan.

Pliable clay in the potter's hand is in no position to question the wisdom of the potter's mental plan. Neither does it know fully what that plan is, nor does it have the power to realign the potter's thinking if it did know. Pliable clay simply submits to the wisdom of the potter.

The Bible alludes to this several times. Isaiah warns, "Woe unto him that striveth with his Maker! Let the potsherd strive with the potsherds of the earth. Shall the clay say to him that fashioneth it, What makest thou? . . ." (Isa.. 45:9). Paul rephrases this, "Shall the thing formed say to him that formed it, Why hast thou made me thus?" (Rom. 9:20). See also Isaiah 29:16.

When the clay does not question why the potter has chosen a certain design for it, this reflects a particular attitude. It is the attitude of pliability. Pliability is the opposite of inflexibility. There's a brilliant example of this attitude in one of our favorite parables of Jesus. It is the parable of the prodigal son.

In this delightful parable a certain man had two sons (Luke 15:11-32). The younger son demanded of his father, saying, "Father, give me the portion of goods that falleth to me" (vs. 12). As a result of this "Give Me" demand, the father decided to divide his inheritance between both sons.

You know the story. The younger son left home in a huff. He squandered away his inheritance and was soon caught in a famine. He decided he had to return to his father, with his tail between his legs, and confess what a fool he had been. When he approached his loving father, he vowed to confess, "Father, I have sinned against heaven, and before thee" (vs. 18). This is a far cry from his original "Give Me" demand. When he said, "I have sinned," in essence he was saying, "Forgive Me," and a "Forgive Me" confession beats a "Give Me" demand any day.

But that's not the end of the parable. Asking for forgiveness may show repentance, but it doesn't show pliability, and pliability is the key to usability. Thus the son made one additional request. He said, "Make me as one of thy hired servants" (vs. 19). That's pliability. From "Give Me" to "Forgive Me" is fine, and necessary, but usability begins when we go from "Forgive Me" to "Make Me." Have you come to that point in your Christian experience?

As pliable clay, we do not question the plan or workmanship of our Potter. After all, He is the omniscient God, and even more, He is our loving Father. There's no reason to question one who knows what's best for us and loves us dearly. We wisely accept His plan for our lives.

The Potter Remolds the Clay as He Wills

Occasionally the potter chooses to remold the same lump of clay. As he had power over it the first time, while it was moist and soft, he has power over it the second time. This teaches us another truth about pliability.

There is an exceedingly tender passage of Scripture recorded by the prophet Jeremiah. It is found in Jeremiah 18:1-6. The Lord spoke to Jeremiah and commanded him to go to a nearby potter's house, for there he would hear the word of the Lord. Jeremiah did so and watched as the potter "wrought a work on the wheels" (vs. 3). What Jeremiah then saw exhibits the grace of God in the most beautiful way.

Jeremiah 18:4 records, "And the vessel that he made of clay was marred in the hand of the potter." It wasn't quite what the potter wanted. The vessel was unfit; it was useless. Had it been allowed to harden, it would have been taken out behind the potter's house and discarded in the potter's field.

But the verse continues, "So he made it again another vessel, as seemed good to the potter to make it." Occasionally a vessel seems to be taking shape on the potter's wheel. But the shape it is taking is not the ultimate design of the potter, and thus with characteristic tenderness he exercises his prerogative to redesign the clay. He takes the same clay and makes it into another vessel as seems good to him.

For the pliable Christian, our Father the Potter frequently does the same thing. I have seen Christians who were successful businessmen one day just walk away from it all to prepare to serve the Lord as a pastor. I have seen Christians quit lucrative careers in engineering, science and high technology to become church planters in some remote village of the world. And how did this happen? The Potter took the pliable clay and made it again another vessel unto His honor. That's what the sovereign Potter will do if He chooses, but only with pliable clay.

Only When the Clay Hardens Is It Breakable

A final truth about the potter and pliable clay relates to hardening. Occasionally one of those potters from Oberbetschdorf would drop a lump of clay on the floor. It would pretty much retain its shape — all but for the bottom. It took the shape of the floor. Without concern the potter would pick up the lump, brush off any impurities, place it on the wheel and continue to fashion it according to his mental plan. Dropping a lump of clay on the floor always had the same result. There was no long-lasting damage as long as the clay was moldable, shapable, pliable.

But once the clay had been placed in the kiln and heated, hardening the earthen vessel, the result would be entirely different. If then such a vessel was dropped to the floor, the result was different but still always the same — scores of broken pieces.

The Bible frequently uses the breaking of clay vessels as a figure of divine judgment (cf. Psalm 2:9; Isa. 30:14; Jer. 19:11). Clay that is moist and soft and pliable can be molded again and again by the potter, but hardened clay can never be molded again. It is destined for the potter's field.

These five truths are basically not about the art of pottery. They are truths about the pliability of people. As a Christian, if I am stubborn, inflexible, unwilling to listen to the still small voice of God, if I am hardened like these vessels of clay, I am destined for the same disposal. As they end up in an earthenware junkyard, so I will end up in an unusable servant junkyard.

Even the Apostle Paul was concerned about this when he said, "But I keep under my body, and bring it into subjection [pliability]: lest that by any means, when I have preached to others, I myself should be a castaway" (1 Cor. 9:27).

The attitude of pliability must never be underestimated with regard to the vanishing ministry. Thousands of lumps of clay right now are refusing to be placed on the Potter's wheel, and thousands more have already been discarded in the Potter's field. It's only in the Potter's hand that we find fulfillment. Oh, to remain in His hand!

When Christians refuse to be pliable in the Master's hand, they are afflicted with a disease I call "hardening of the attitudes." Hardened attitudes toward God and His choices for our life contribute to the vanishing ministry. This is why pliability in every Christian, young or old, is so vital to hearing God's call and obeying His voice.

– 14 –

Risk Taking.

The Attitude of Expendability

In a day when most servants of the Lord are concerned about burnout, you may find it strange that I write about the concept of expendability. But I do so only because the Bible does.

One of the most important attitudes for the lifelong servant of the Lord is the attitude of expendability. Perhaps it is so important because in these last years of the 20th century it is found in diminishing quantities. As this attitude vanishes, so does the ministry.

Expendability is the quality of being used up, of being consumed. It's not a popular attitude in our burnout-conscious society. Burnout is a real problem and should not be minimized. But we must beware of the burnout cop-out, using burnout only as an excuse for reduced effort.

Expendability means we are willing to lay aside our self-interests, lay aside our own desires, lay aside our short-term service plans and give our lives to be expended for the exciting task of winning the world to Christ. We do not cling to our rights and privileges but are willing to relinquish those rights and spend those privileges and be spent personally in the cause of our Lord.

Often in counseling a pastor hears a wife complain, "I was used; he used me for his own purposes, and I never was able to live my own life." None of us naturally wants to be used. We want to be fulfilled in and of ourselves, not used by others. But expendability means exactly that — being used to the fullest by our Saviour, and by and large we don't want that anymore.

We are so quick to say, "You're not going to use me!" that we almost unknowingly respond that way when the Lord tenderly deals with our heart. Instead of, "Yes, Lord, use me. I want to be used by You," we recoil at the very thought. But being used by the Saviour is being fulfilled, giving meaning and purpose to our Christian life.

The prophets of old viewed their lives as something to be totally consumed by God. The prophets of today view their lives as something to be totally enriched by God. That's the difference in our view of expendability, and it's one of the strongest contributing factors in the vanishing ministry.

Let's consider someone who was expendable — someone who viewed his very life as a glowing ember that would be burned up. No, I do not speak of the Lord Jesus, although I could. His strength, His glory and His very life were entirely expended on Calvary's cross. The cry, "It is finished," is more than a cry of victory; it is a cry of accomplishment. He gave His life; it was not snatched from Him. Expendability always gives more than it receives.

Perhaps a more down-to-earth example of expendability is the Apostle Paul. He was expendable, and he liked it that way.

In his second epistle to the Corinthian church Paul was forced to spend much of his letter authenticating his apostleship and justifying his right to instruct a church that he had founded in the first place. This shouldn't have been necessary, but frequently things become necessary that shouldn't be.

You can clearly read the pathos in his voice when he writes to the Corinthian believers, "Behold, the third time I am ready to come to you" (2 Cor. 12:14). There was no sacrifice too great to be made in the cause of Christ. Paul even has to promise that he will not be burdensome to the Corinthians and then exclaims, "For I seek not yours, but you."

How it must have crushed his heart to have his motives misjudged by the very people he led to the Lord and established in the faith. Paul wasn't after their money. He was after them. He said, "I seek not yours, but you" (2 Cor. 12:14). He wasn't interested in their things; he was interested in them. He wasn't looking to be appreciated by them; he was looking to be expended for them.

In fact, that is exactly what he says to them. Verse 15 reads, "And I will very gladly spend and be spent for you." He has labored with a pure heart, with no ulterior motives. In proof of that he is willing to be entirely consumed for them. He is willing to burn out for them. He is willing to die for them. And he would do so gladly.

The word translated "be spent" means exactly that. Paul was willing to be expendable for the cause of Christ at Corinth. He did not want a church named after him. He did not want the Corinthians' praise. He clearly wanted the Corinthians themselves, and he was willing to be consumed for their sakes.

Being expendable means giving without getting. We naturally repel the idea that we would give our lives and get no recognition, no praise, no adulation in return. But our blood would boil if we felt we had given with no thanksgiving in return. Yet, that is exactly what Paul knew would be the case at Corinth.

Having noted that he was expendable and would even gladly be spent for them, Paul observes, "Though the more abundantly I love you, the less I be loved" (2 Cor. 12:15). He was willing to die for them; they weren't willing even to love him for it.

One of the most difficult lessons I have to teach young pastors is the more expendable the shepherd is for the sheep, frequently the less appreciated he is by the sheep. You say, "It isn't fair!" Right, it isn't fair. So? The Master didn't call us to expend our lives to perpetuate a fairness doctrine. He called us to be ignitable torches, willing to burn brightly for Him until our flame is extinguished by time or unfair circumstances, and our willingness to be consumed will largely determine our willingness to answer the call to lifetime service.

The attitude of expendability. To be used of God and by God. To lay your life on the line and say, "Here it is Lord. I want my brief life span to be spent!" After all, our Father isn't asking anything of us that He hasn't already asked of His own dear Son. There is no difference in His request. The difference may be only in our response.

The trouble with being expendable is that God may indeed expend you. Those five brave missionaries killed by the Auca Indians in 1956 are not best characterized by bravery. They are not best characterized by availability. They are best characterized by the attitude of expendability. And they were spent!

If Jim Elliott, Nate Saint or any of the others were called back from Glory today and asked whether they would lay their lives on the line again, what do you suppose they would say? That's the attitude of expendability. It is a missing attitude among most Christians today.

Remember Jim Elliott's own words: "He is no fool who gives up what he cannot keep to gain what he cannot lose." Expendability!

– 15 –

The Attitude of Ownership

I've saved this attitude until last. It is the attitude upon which all the others rise or fall. We can be committed, we can be compassionate, we can be pliable and expendable, but these are all based on one attitude — the attitude of ownership.

One of the basic questions of the Christian's life is, "Who's in charge?" The honest answer to that question could spell an immediate turnaround for the vanishing ministry.

Ownership is a concept with which we have become quite familiar. We own cars — "It's my car!" We own clothes — "How do you like her sweater?" We own houses — "It's the bank's and mine!" We own businesses — "He's in business for himself." In fact, we have little or no aversion to the concept of ownership, as long as it doesn't apply to us — "You don't own me!"

But that's the point. The Bible says it does apply to us. Until we grasp what that means and internalize it into our thinking about lifetime service, the vanishing ministry will continue.

At the start there must be a distinction made between ownership and authority. Some people have authority over other people, but they don't own them. Remember the story of the centurion in Matthew 8.

Jesus had just entered Capernaum when a centurion rushed up to Him. The centurion's servant was ill and grievously tormented. He had come to Jesus to seek healing for the miserable servant. The Lord offered to come to his house, but in humility the centurion begged off. To show Jesus that he understood authority, that Jesus had authority just to speak a word of healing without coming to the house, the centurion said, "For I am a man under authority, having soldiers under me: and I say to this man, Go, and he goeth; and to another, Come, and he cometh; and to my servant, Do this, and he doeth it" (Matt. 8:9).

That's authority. The authority of a superior permits him to order others and expect his orders to be carried out. He says, "Do this" and the servant does it because he is a servant. His master speaks with authority, not ownership.

It is true that Jesus Christ is our Master. He is our Lord. He speaks with authority. He says, "Go" and we go; "Stay" and we stay. But that is all based upon His authority. Authority alone should be sufficient to cause us to do the bidding of the Lord. But if it isn't, there is even greater motivation. Not only does He order us, but He owns us as well.

Ownership is frequently seen in the Bible. But to be valid, ownership must be obtained in a proper manner. One of the guidelines for ownership is that it must be expressed publicly. Anytime something was purchased, it was purchased in full view of a watching world.

When Boaz performed the rite of the near kinsman and purchased the inheritance of Elimelech and his two sons, he took great pains to do so in the public eye. Ruth 4:9 reveals, "And Boaz said unto the elders, and unto all the people, Ye are witnesses this day that I have bought all that was Elimelech's, and all that was Chilion's and Mahlon's, of the hand of Naomi." To be binding, purchase must be public.

There's more. Purchases made in Bible times always required the recording of a deed or sealing of a contract. They were not proper if they were not sealed. Even those that took place with just a handshake ultimately were recorded at the gate of the city.

Jeremiah the prophet was in prison in King Zedekiah's house. He had prophesied of the destruction of Jerusalem, and that got him into trouble with the king. While imprisoned, his uncle's son came to him, requesting that he buy a field in Anathoth. Jeremiah agreed and recorded, "And I subscribed the evidence, and sealed it, and took witnesses, and weighed him the money in the balances . . . and I gave the evidence of the purchase unto Baruch . . . in the presence of the witnesses that subscribed the book of the purchase, before all the Jews that sat in the court of the prison" (Jer. 32:10-12). To be binding, then, a purchase must be made in public and signed and sealed in public.

There's still more. A price must be paid for a purchase or it was invalid. Without a price paid it would not be a purchase but a gift. Ownership has to cost the owner something. Two examples immediately come to mind.

When Abraham wanted to buy the cave of Machpelah as a burial place for his beloved Sarah, Genesis 23:13 records, "And he spake unto Ephron in the audience of the people of the land, saying, But if thou wilt give it, I pray thee, hear me: I will give thee money for the field." Ephron recognized Abraham to be a rich man as himself and offered simply to make the parcel a gift. Abraham refused and "weighed to Ephron the silver, which he had named in the audience of the sons of Heth, four hundred shekels of silver, current money with the merchant" (Gen. 23:16). To be binding, a price had to be paid.

And what of David when he purchased the threshingfloor of Araunah the Jebusite? Araunah asked the king why he had come, and David replied, "To buy the threshingfloor of thee, to build an altar unto the LORD" (2 Sam. 24:21). Araunah objected. How could he take money from the king, from God's anointed?

But David objected more strenuously. "And the king said unto Araunah, Nay; but I will surely buy it of thee at a price: neither will I offer burnt offerings unto the LORD my God of that which doth cost me nothing" (2 Sam. 24:24). To be binding, a price had to be paid.

Any transaction which was deemed legitimate occurred publicly, was recorded and sealed properly, and was as a result of a price being paid.

Now, don't read on until you see clearly that this is exactly what transpired when Jesus Christ died for us. His death at Calvary purchased our atonement from sin. It was accomplished publicly. The ugly mob that day cried for his public execution. They spat upon Him, mocked Him, ridiculed Him, beat upon Him "and sitting down they watched him there" (Matt. 27:36).

Not only was our atonement purchased publicly, but it was sealed and recorded properly. Begging for Jehovah to forgive His wayward people, Moses pleaded with God either to forgive their great sin or, if that were not possible, "blot me, I pray thee, out of thy book which thou hast written" (Exod. 32:32). Of him who overcomes the Lord said, "I will not blot out his name out of the book of life" (Rev. 3:5). Jesus told the disciples to rejoice "because your names are written in heaven" (Luke 10:20). Yes, because the blood of Jesus Christ has been applied to my sinful life, my name is written down in the Lamb's book of life and shall never be blotted out. I am His purchased possession, and it has been recorded properly and sealed by His Holy Spirit (Eph. 1:13).

The atonement for my sin was made publicly and recorded properly, but also it required that a price be paid. That price was not the 30 pieces of silver Judas received for betraying the Lord Jesus. That price was the blood of Jesus Christ Himself.

The Bible makes this amply clear. In his letter to the Colossians Paul reminds us to give thanks to God the Father because: (1) He made us fit to receive the inheritance of saints; (2) He delivered us from the power of darkness; (3) He translated us into the kingdom of His dear Son; and (4) He provided the forgiveness of sins through the Son "in whom we have redemption through his blood" (Col. 1:12-14).

As believers, we are more than happy to accept all of this. We anticipate our inheritance, we walk in the light, we enjoy His kingdom promise, and we rejoice in the fact that we are His purchased possession.

And then we discover the other side of the coin. Then we have it brought to our attention that the Lord Jesus paid a very dear price for us so we could be His possession. Then we remember that possessions are expendable and can be used up at the will of the owner. Then we remember that He owns us. And that's where the rub comes. He owns us!

Earlier I mentioned that I was frequently invited as a speaker at the graduation ceremonies of Christian high schools. I enjoyed doing this and always asked for some time alone with the seniors. I used to say to them, "In the next few weeks you will be asked one question again and again — 'What do you want to do with your life?'"

That seems like a legitimate question — especially when young people are facing a choice of colleges and careers. But I was quick to remind these Christian young people that God didn't really care what they wanted to do with their life. He didn't save them so they could do with their life what they wanted to do. He saved them so He could do with their life what He wanted to do. It's a question of ownership.

Paul reminds the Corinthian Christians what every man, woman, teenager and child today who claims Jesus Christ as Saviour needs to be reminded of. "Ye are not your own. For ye are bought with a price!" (1 Cor. 6:19-20). Christ Jesus redeemed us publicly. Our salvation was recorded in His own blood in the book of life. He paid the dearest price possible for us. What makes us think we can ignore what our Owner desires of us and get away with it?

Young people today should never consider a career based on their likes or interests. Still, most Christian young people use that and the amount of money they can make as their only criteria for a career. They have been bought with the blood of Christ but haven't had the courtesy to seek His will in choosing a career. They have never learned the attitude of ownership.

Would my Master call me to a career that I had no interest in? Absolutely. He did that for Paul. Paul was a persecutor of the church and injurious toward it. God called Him to be a church planter, the farthest thing from Paul's mind. But God can change our minds, when we have the mind of Christ.

Would my Master call me to serve Him in a place I didn't want to go? Absolutely. Read the way the Sovereign God treated the wishes of His servants Paul and Timothy. "Now when they had gone throughout Phrygia and the region of Galatia, and were forbidden of the Holy Ghost to preach the word in Asia, after they were come to Mysia, they assayed to go into Bithynia: but the Spirit suffered them not. And they passing by Mysia came down to Troas" (Acts 16:6-8).

Where did we ever get the idea that God formulates His plan for our lives based on our goals and interests? Who is the real god here? We are not our own, we are bought with a price and that means ownership. I do not do what I want. I do not formulate my life's plans based on my interests. He owns me, and I am happy only when my wants and interests are molded into His.

On January 12, 1722, Jonathan Edwards, whose preaching brought about the first Great Awakening in America, wrote in his diary: "I have been before God, and have given myself, all that I am and have, to God; so that I am not, in any respect, my own . . . . Neither have any right to this body or any of its members — no right to this tongue, these hands, these feet; no right to these senses, these eyes, these ears, this smell, or this taste. I have given myself clear away and have not retained any thing as my own."

Edwards penned those words when he was a 19-year-old student. He was giving His life to the Lord, for he had settled the question of ownership. After this God used him to stir a whole nation and assume the presidency of Princeton University, all for the glory of God.

Much of the vanishing ministry question would be solved immediately if Christians would solve the ownership question. Who's in charge? When we can answer that honestly and act accordingly, I suspect the whitened fields will have more laborers in them.

The attitudes of lifetime servants must be present in you and me, or we will confuse God's still small voice for our own inner voice of desire. The attitudes of lifetime servants must be present in you and me or the vanishing ministry will continue to vanish, and we will do the worst thing possible — nothing. Examine yourself for the fingerprints of God and for the attitudes of service.

Conclusion

There is an undeniable link between the company of the committed and the number of lifetime servants in the Lord's vineyard. Although there will no doubt be some who will read this and argue that Christians cannot be blamed if God does not call them to lifetime service, it appears that the lack of proper attitudes toward lifetime service is a greater deterrent than the lack of God's call.

When men and women are right before God, the call of God seems to come with greater frequency. It has nothing whatever to do with whether or not God wants workers; as long as the laborers are few, God wants workers. It has everything to do with right hearts and right attitudes toward the call of God.

Yale University's campus was rife with infidelity and rebellion when Timothy Dwight became the new president in 1795. Born of good Puritan preaching stock, Dwight was the grandson of Jonathan Edwards. Describing Yale before President Dwight was inaugurated, Lyman Beecher noted, "Before he came, college was in a most ungodly state . . . . Most of the students were skeptical, and rowdies were plenty."

Into this den of infidelity walked a man concerned with the spiritual welfare of his students. Initially Dwight fired all faculty members who espoused French Rationalism. Then he reasoned the faith with skeptical students. On Sundays he preached hard against sin and the student's insensitivity to the things of God. Timothy Dwight never let up. He would not permit Yale students to equivocate. They would serve either God or Baal.

Still, few students made professions of faith in Christ during President Dwight's first years. Finally, in 1802, his efforts paid off and revival fell upon Yale as they had never seen before or since. In March a student was saved and another in April. By the end of the summer there were more than 50 students who had come to Christ. And salvation wasn't the end.

By the time the senior class was ready to graduate, half of them had committed their lives to Christ and a third of them had committed their lives to lifetime service to Christ.

Hear me well! Revival always swells the ranks of lifetime servants for the Lord. If the ranks are depleted today, the attitudes listed above need to be implemented in our lives. That in itself is revival, and there has never been a revival without a corresponding flood of laborers for the vineyard. And therein lies the key to turning about the vanishing ministry.

Ministry ranks are not decreasing because God isn't calling sufficient men and women to serve Him. Ministry ranks are decreasing because Christians are suffering from hardening of the attitudes. When God's people experience personal revival and are right with Him, there won't be a need for recruiting soldiers. The volunteers will overwhelm us.

Part Four
The Road Back

Where do we go from here?

The Road Back

Where do we go from here?

The need is real. The road back will address that need, or there will be no road back.

Presently 4,000 to 5,000 openings for full-time missionaries need to be filled among North American Protestant mission agencies. That's just to keep pace; and if we just keep pace, we lose the battle anyway.

The road back is a treacherous one. It is likely to be resisted by well-meaning Christians. Those who fail to see that a problem exists will also fail to see the need for a road back. But their lack of belief in the truth does not negate the truth. Truth is truth, whether they believe it or not.

If we are to raise up another generation of champions for Christ, who will be on the road back helping to do that? If we are to provide sufficient candidates for the empty pulpits of America, who will be on the road back giving gentle guidance? If we are to finance the missionary enterprise to any extent that can be considered adequate, whose pockets will be opened? If God does ask this generation, "Whom shall I send, and who will go for us?", who will respond affirmatively?

If we're going to get back, let's see who's on the road back.

– 16 –

Heritage Parents

If the vanishing ministry is to be recovered it will have to begin at the cradle. Christian parents who love their children must love them the way God the Father loved His Son — by giving them.

In our society the child has become like a two-liter container of Pepsi. He is small enough to be held in our arms. He is usually colorfully wrapped. He can be the hit of the party. He can also be placed in day storage awaiting the arrival of his parents from work each evening. But most of all, if Mommy and Daddy don't want him, they can dispose of him properly. In fact, Pepsi bottles and fetuses have been found in the same trash bins in America.

I don't believe abortion is an option for a Christian. But many Christian parents who would never dream of aborting their children physically will not hesitate to deprive them of the right kind of spiritual life. This usually happens when Christian parents have an inappropriate attitude toward their children, and they probably don't even know it.

Psalm 127:3 makes abundantly clear what our attitude toward our children ought to be. "Lo, children are an heritage of the Lord." That is, our children, all of our children, are on loan to us from the bank of heaven. We have been charged with the stewardship of raising them.

Our children are just like the talents in the parable of the talents in Matthew 25. They are small when given to us, but through proper care and feeding they grow, and at the end of our stewardship we have a matured talent to give back to the Master, with interest. But this growth is not just physical; it is spiritual as well.

It is important that my children get a well-balanced diet so they grow properly. They must have a good mixture of proteins, dairy, carbohydrates and more. Likewise, they need a well-balanced spiritual diet. They must have a good mixture of Psalms, Deuteronomy, Corinthians and more. This is my responsibility as their parent, in both cases.

Having invested much time in the talents entrusted to him, one of the most difficult things for the steward to remember is that those talents do not actually belong to him. He is just charged with their care and maturity. They are owned by another.

Having invested much time in the children entrusted to us, one of the most difficult things for the parent to remember is that those children do not actually belong to us. We are just charged with their care and maturity. They are owned by another.

"Children are an heritage of the Lord" means that they are His children, not ours. Yes, they have Daddy's eyes and Mommy's nose, but they bear God's image. They are His children and are to be raised by us for His purposes, not ours.

Perhaps the classic example of this attitude toward children is seen in a godly mother named Eunice who was the mother of Timothy.

We know little or nothing of her except that she was a Jewess and a believer in Christ, but she was married to an unbelieving Greek (Acts 16:1).

Paul tells us that her mother, Lois, and she raised Timothy in the faith, though Timothy did not come to trust Christ until years later. Both Grandma Lois and Mother Eunice saw to it that young Timothy was taught the Scriptures as a lad. When the apostle cautioned Timothy to continue in the things he had learned "knowing of whom thou hast learned them" (2 Tim. 3:14), he was not warning Timothy that much of his time and effort had gone into the lad and the apostle did not want that effort to be wasted after he was gone.

Actually the next verse tells who is the one from whom Timothy had learned the Word. "And that from a child thou hast known the holy scriptures, which are able to make thee wise unto salvation through faith which is in Christ Jesus" (2 Tim. 3:15). Timothy had been taught the Holy Scriptures from his mother's knee and probably on his mother's knee. Eunice had invested well the talent committed to her.

Because she had an unbelieving husband, you can imagine how much it meant to Eunice when Timothy came to know the Lord as Saviour. She probably was justly proud of him when the brethren at Lystra and Iconium commended her son to Paul as one worthy of lifetime service to the Lord. But therein comes the rub.

Paul came to Lystra looking for a young travel companion on his second missionary journey. When it became evident that Timothy was the man (Acts 16:1-3), do you know what Eunice said when Paul indicated he wanted Timothy to leave home for ministry? Do you know what she said? Nothing! Why should she? That's why she raised Timothy. He was an heritage of the Lord; he belonged to the Lord. This was her opportunity to give back to the Master the talent He had committed unto her to invest.

Did Eunice have any maternal feelings about Timothy's entering the lifetime ministry? Probably. Did she shed some heartfelt tears? Undoubtedly. Did she have some motherly advice? Unquestionably. But the bottom line is still the same. Children are an heritage of the Lord. Parents rightly raise them when they raise their children for Him and His purpose.

Many young people today do not have doors of service open to them because a well-meaning mother has been hiding her children in a closet marked "Business" or "Education" just so she can keep them. In fact, it is impossible to keep our children, but it is possible to give them to the Lord.

A couple of summers ago Paul Bubar, Overseas Director for Word of Life, interviewed about 20 kids each week at Word of Life Island, their teen camp. He asked, "If you could be anything you wanted to be, what would you be?" The responses ranged from architects to veterinarians. "Out of the entire summer," said Bubar, "only one said, 'I want to be a youth pastor.' None said, 'I want to be a pastor,' and three said, 'I want to be a missionary.' Each week I asked how many came from homes where both parents were saved. The figure was an astounding 81percent. This tells me that Christian parents, in their quest for their children to have financial security in life, have held up all these secular options. Very few are holding up service to the Lord as an option. In my opinion, kids are not being urged to serve the Lord in a full-time capacity."

I am the middle of three sons. Both my brothers are also involved in ministry. One day someone asked my parents how it happened that all three of their sons ended up in the gospel ministry. My parents didn't have a ready answer. Since I overheard the question, I volunteered an answer. I said, "My parents never forced me into ministry. They just made sure as I was growing up that every time I turned around there was an open door of service." I am convinced that my father and mother went around the night before opening doors of service that I knew nothing about. That's why they raised me.

We parents must recognize the mark of God on "His" children right from the cradle. We must recognize our right relationship to them, and to Him. We must view them as His heritage, on loan to us to invest our lives in. We must prepare for and anticipate that day when He chooses to use our children because we have been faithful in raising them.

The vanishing ministry will not vanish so rapidly if well-meaning Christian parents would stop hiding their children from God. Let's be heritage parents, parents who recognize that our children are an heritage of the Lord. Let's tithe our children as we do our money. And if He chooses not to use them in a lifetime ministry, we will not breathe a sigh of relief but will rejoice that the Master has done with our talent what most pleases Him.

My greatest gift to God, beyond myself, is my children. As God gave His Son for me, I must give my son and daughters to Him. They are in good hands. Together we are on the road back.

– 17 –

Barnabas Pastors

One of the key players on the road back is the pastor. Together the senior pastor of a church and the youth pastor can have as much spiritual impact on the career goals of young church members as anyone. Still, many pastors frequently abdicate this cherished position.

The role described below is one that must be assumed and aggressively pursued by concerned pastors if the vanishing ministry is to be halted.

Earlier I referred to the Eli Syndrome, where a pastor is insensitive to the call of God in the life of his young Samuels. Happily not all biblical leaders are of this type. Take, for example, Barnabas.

In Acts 11 this Christian leader clearly assumed five different roles. The first was *ambassador* (vs. 22). When Grecians became believers at Antioch, the church of Jerusalem sent Barnabas as an ambassador to the church of Antioch to inquire of the propriety of receiving Greeks into their fellowship. The second role played by Barnabas was *exhorter* (vs. 23). He challenged the believers of Antioch to continue in one accord and hold fast to the Saviour.

Barnabas' third role was *example* (vs. 24). It is said of him that he was "a good man, and full of the Holy Ghost and of faith." His very character was an encouragement to the church. The fourth role he assumed was *teacher* (vs. 26).

For a solid year Barnabas conducted Bible classes for the Christians at the Antioch church.

But the role played by Barnabas that we rarely recognize was *recruiter* (vs. 25). Barnabas was a premier recruiter for the cause of Christ. After all, he recruited the Apostle Paul, an accomplishment not without some significance.

Of course, Barnabas was not the first recruiter for lifetime ministry. Precedent had been set some years before. When Andrew followed John the Baptist and heard the forerunner say of Jesus Christ, "Behold the Lamb of God, which taketh away the sin of the world" (John 1:29), his first official role as a believer was that of recruiter. John 1:41-42 records, "He first findeth his own brother Simon, and saith unto him, We have found the Messias, which is, being interpreted the Christ. And he brought him to Jesus."

The same was true of Philip. The day after the call of Peter and Andrew to lifetime ministry the Saviour was walking along the shores of the sea of Galilee when He encountered Philip and said, "Follow me." The initial response of Philip was classic. "Philip findeth Nathanael, and saith unto him, We have found him, of whom Moses in the law, and the prophets, did write, Jesus of Nazareth, the son of Joseph" (John 1:45).

It may be argued that Andrew and Philip weren't recruiters as much as they were evangelists. But aren't recruitment and evangelism the same? Do we not recruit when we evangelize? We recruit for service as the normal and immediate consequence of salvation (Eph. 2:8-10).

Be that as it may, in the case of Barnabas he was certainly not recruiting Paul to salvation but to service. After Paul's salvation on the road to Damascus he went immediately to the house of Judas in Damascus where the ministry of Ananias restored sight to him. Afterward Paul must have made his trip into Arabia and returned to Damascus. It was after three years (in Damascus, not in Arabia—see Galatians 1:17-18) that Paul's preaching stirred up the Jews of Damascus, and he was whisked away by night on his journey to Jerusalem. But the Jerusalem believers still feared Paul, whom they knew as Saul of Tarsus (Acts 9:26), and thus it was Barnabas who brought Paul to the apostles so they could verify his conversion.

Once the genuineness of Paul's conversion and call to ministry was established, Luke records, "And he spake boldly in the name of the Lord Jesus, and disputed against the Grecians: but they went about to slay him" (Acts 9:29). To spare his life, the brethren brought Paul down to the harbor at Caesarea and sent him sailing for his hometown of Tarsus. Here Paul matured and blossomed as a believer and a preacher in preparation for the day he would be greatly used of God.

When it became evident to Barnabas that the ministry in Antioch was more than he could manage singlehandedly, he decided to do what every sensitive man of God does when he sees a need. Barnabas' thoughts turned toward recruiting additional help. Whom would he get? This person would have to be gifted and spiritually mature. He would have to have all the essential attitudes for lifetime ministry described in the previous part of this book. Did he know anyone like that?

Acts 11:25-26 records Barnabas' solution to his problem. "Then departed Barnabas to Tarsus, for to seek Saul: and when he had found him, he brought him unto Antioch." Notice how much discussion there was on whether or not Paul wanted to come. Notice, too, how long Paul deliberated whether or not he should come. Undoubtedly they prayed about it and maybe even fasted (see Acts 13:1-2), but there is little discussion or deliberation when there is work to be done. Those saved to serve don't deliberate long; they just get busy.

Barnabas recruited Paul for ministry. He could have prayed that God would send someone to help him in the ministry at Antioch. Undoubtedly he did pray. But meaningful prayer requires purposeful action. Barnabas prayed and recruited.

Somehow we have apparently come to believe in the 20th century that to recruit for ministry is spiritually akin to campaigning for a pastorate. It's not something we should do but something God will take care of!

Moses' servant and spiritual understudy was a young man named Joshua, introduced to us first in Exodus 17. Where do you suppose Moses got Joshua? Do you suppose Joshua latched onto Moses or the other way around? I think Moses recruited Joshua.

After Elijah's contest with the prophets of Baal and his suspect behavior under the juniper tree, God spoke to the prophet through that still small voice. We all know that God chose not to speak in the strong wind, the earthquake or the fire, but do we know what God said to Elijah when He spoke in the still small voice? What was Elijah commanded to do?

The prophet was told to anoint three persons. First, he must anoint Hazael to be king of Syria. Then he must anoint Jehu to be king of Israel. And finally, he must anoint Elisha to be a prophet of God. That's as close to recruitment as you can get in prophetic history.

Did Paul recruit young Timothy when the apostle arrived at Derbe and Lystra? Absolutely! Did Barnabas recruit Saul when he arrived in Tarsus? Absolutely! Do we actively recruit men and women from our church youth groups to ministry? Probably not! Pastors will either actively recruit young Joshuas, young Elishas, young Timothys or older Sauls from their congregation, or they will simply lament the fact that the fields are so white while the laborers are so few. Pastors who are not part of the solution are the alternative.

And what about you, pastor? Are you a lamenter or a recruiter? Are you a Barnabas pastor? Do you view recruitment of soldiers as part of your role as commander, or are you willing to limp along with inadequate troops because that's "somebody else's job"? Moses, Elijah and Barnabas all viewed it as their job. But more than that, it was their challenging privilege.

Perhaps the greatest recruitment burden lies on the youth pastor or youth sponsors in the local church. Here is where the best recruitment takes place. If the vanishing ministry is to be halted and the army to make a comeback, youth pastors must shed their devalued opinion of their own contribution to the life of the church. Recruiting young men and women for ministry out of your youth group is the life of the church. That's a powerful responsibility.

The joys and rewards of lifetime ministry ought ever to be kept before young people in our churches. The needs of the whitened fields ought to be constantly before their eyes. The burden of the youth pastor for unreached teenagers in the community ought to be real and transparent. The opportunities for active participation in the worship and praise services of the church ought to be frequent. Meaningful and fun outreach ministries ought to be consistent and staffed with the church's key youth. But most of all, opportunities for commitment to lifetime service ought to be often and impressive.

Perhaps if we kept meaningful and fruitful opportunities for ministry before our young people, if we opted out of the theme park scene and the extravaganzas into which we try to weave a ten-minute devotional and replaced them with solid and sincere service to the Lord, we would see the fire of the heart spread to the next generation.

What is a Barnabas pastor? He is a pastor who, like Barnabas, recognizes that recruitment for ministry is not unspiritual. A Barnabas pastor is one who, like Barnabas, recognizes that recruitment for ministry is not unscriptural. A Barnabas pastor is one who, like Barnabas, teaches and exhorts but recognizes that two servants are better than one.

The Barnabas pastor looks back on his life and ministry with considerable satisfaction, for he sees a little of himself in the ministry of each of his Pauls. His ministry extends around the world in the ministries of those he recruited from his congregation.

If we are to come back, the road back must find innumerable pastors on it committed to recruitment like Barnabas was. How about it, pastor? Nobody else has your opportunity.

– 18 –

Ministry Education

Because ministry education has seriously slipped from its original prominence both in evangelical and liberal institutions, some hard questions must be asked by college and seminary trustees, administrators and faculty. After all, inasmuch as the road to where we are is littered with the carcasses of institutions which once were primarily pastoral training schools and are now something else, it is likely that the road back will be littered with the carcasses of institutions which now are something else but have returned to their original ministry mission.

The strength of ministry training in our institutions of higher education will reflect to some extent the strength of our churches. The local church should be the prime recruiter for ministry, not the Christian college. But once the church has recruited for ministry, it is essential that the Christian college not sidetrack that budding pastor or missionary into some other field.

For this reason churches should exert more influence on colleges and seminaries, especially if they support such schools with their dollars. Pastor, do you know what percentage of your gifts to the college of your choice are actually used to prepare students for ministry? If not, do you know how to find out?

After all, why would a church send money designated for missions to a college in which only fifteen or twenty percent or less of the student body was preparing for ministry? Why would a church send mission budget dollars to support a huge athletic program or purchase sophisticated microscopes for the science department or new computers for the business department? Is that what support from local churches is designed to underwrite? If not, why do you support the college of your choice?

I question this only to lay the foundation for those important questions trustees must ask themselves. Christian colleges may need athletic programs, sophisticated microscopes or business computers. That's not the point.

The point is this. Many educational institutions which once enjoyed church support because they were primarily an educational arm of the local church are today church-related at best and entirely unconcerned with the church at worst. Many institutions which once displayed a level of concern for taking the gospel to every corner of the globe, this concern being evidenced by the number of pastoral and missions majors they had, today display their level of concern in a similar and depressing fashion—the lack of pastoral and missions majors. It should be disheartening to church supporters.

If an educational institution is to be worthy of church or denominational support, if it is to assist in the task of training an army of soldiers for the cause of Christ, if it is not to be a roadblock on the road back, then what must such institutions do? I have addressed what pastors must do: what now must our Christian colleges do?

A first step in determining whether the health of a person is in jeopardy is to determine what the danger signs are to that person's health. Similarly, if an institution which once had a strong program of ministry is to maintain a viable pastoral training program, what are the danger signs for which we must be vigilant? For the benefit of college trustees, administrators, faculties and supporters, I list seven danger signs to watch out for.

1. There is a danger for pastoral training when the institutional community at large, and the board of control in particular, demonstrates little understanding of or commitment to the institution's historic mission. If the board of trustees cannot articulate to others what their college is all about, what guidance can they give to the institution?

2. There is danger for pastoral training when diversification in curriculum and programs threatens the institution's distinctive mission. In a monograph entitled, "Preserving the Private College—and Diversity," Dr. Mel Scarlett lists 15 danger signs for the private college and prominent among them is "if the institution has precipitously and drastically departed from its basic mission because of financial exigency."[1] In other words, any change in curriculum or programs for the sake of attracting more diverse student interests in order to generate more tuition income is a threat to the distinctive mission of the institution.

3. There is danger for pastoral training when the definition of "ministry" becomes so broad that it includes any vocation pursued by a Christian. Although it is true that every member of God's family is to be about the family business, it is nonetheless true that some are called to live by the ministry. Historically the word "ministry" has related somehow to God's Word instead of His world in general. Today, however, the word is loosely used so that students preparing to be basketball coaches, investment counselors, teachers, social workers or computer programers are said to be preparing for the "ministry." This definition does damage to the historic meaning of the word.

4. There is danger for pastoral training when college presidents continually feature pastoral majors in financial appeals to their church constituency when business, education or other majors have actually supplanted the pastoral major in institutional importance. College presidents know that you can't raise funds from churches or Christian people by featuring a business major. So, most of the appeals you and I receive highlight the pastoral or missions student. But when the number of pastoral majors in an institution is only a small fraction of the total enrollment, it is ethically questionable to mislead the public into believing that the young preacher in the appeal letter or magazine ad is a typical student at that institution.

5. There is danger for pastoral training when the number of required Bible and ministry hours is reduced to accommodate other necessary curricular offerings. When the curriculum committee of a Christian college begins to doubt the necessity for the minimum Bible

requirements or deems other curricular offerings to be of equal or more importance than those Bible requirements, this softening of commitment to the basics of Bible training usually reflects planting the seeds for a de facto change in institutional mission. This is historical reality.

6. There is danger for pastoral training when institutions view themselves simply as preparatory to higher forms of education. Although a young pastor should pursue all the education the Lord will allow, there is just no evidence that his success in ministry depends upon graduate education. It is still the Spirit of God who makes us fruitful. At some point there are certain essentials for ministry that must be learned. To learn them in college without the benefit of graduate education is infinitely better than to have the benefit of graduate education and never learn them.

7. There is danger for pastoral training when administrators are willing to budget high-ticket items to support general education courses but are not willing to budget a proportionately equitable amount to pastoral training. More and more tools of education are super sophisticated, not to mention super expensive. Science labs, computer labs, language labs, a fleet of maxi-vans, a fully equipped weight room, an entire bassoon band — you name it and we've got to have it. But is a preaching lab less necessary than a science lab? Which bears greater eternal rewards? It is easy for this important vocational ministry to get lost in the money maze.

Is it possible that while education has become more technological, more advanced, more sophisticated, that it has also become more eternally obsolete and useless? Our answer will depend on whether or not everything we do is done with the judgment seat of Christ in mind.

Avoiding the dangers listed above will mean those who are committed to Christian education must review the mission statement of their institution to see if they are accomplishing what the founders intended. If not, is what is being accomplished a higher eternal goal than the founder's or a lesser eternal goal? If it is a lesser goal, trustee, administrator, teacher, why do you accept it?

– 19 –

Aggressive Churches

If we really believe that the local church is God's ordained agency for world evangelism, then we should take more seriously the church's role in heading off the vanishing ministry. That role isn't just important; it's central!

The road back does not begin in seminary. The road back does not begin at Urbana. The road back to a vibrant corps of servant/soldiers begins in Christian homes and local churches. There are several avenues our churches can, indeed must, pursue to get us on the road back. Notice what they are.

Recruitment of Members

The institution I served as president for a decade was one dedicated solely to training pastors, missionaries and Christian lay leaders. We had mission agencies on our campus every day, sometimes as many as three a day, recruiting our seniors for their agency. As exciting as that was, this recruitment was to a specific field and a specific agency. It was not recruitment for ministry in general. That had to take place years earlier.

The best, most natural, most biblical place for such recruitment to take place is the local church. Today the church has for the most part handed the recruitment task by default to the Christian college, the student missions conference, the para-church organization. Perhaps the reason is that the church is legitimately busy with other things. After all, there are souls to be saved, building specs to be approved, the annual Sunday school contest to be planned and that squeaky-wheel church member to be appeased. But if recruitment for ministry has become such a low priority, it's no wonder the mess of reality is what it is.

What institution places a young man or young woman in such a conducive environment to be called to ministry as the local church? What institution brings men and women to spiritual choices on such a consistent basis? What institution is a better support group for those tender toward ministry?

What the swamp is to the mosquito, the church is to the missionary. The entire environment of the swamp is conducive to hatching mosquitoes. All the right ingredients are there. Everybody knows if you want to hatch a mosquito, you go to the swamp. Does the local church enjoy a similar reputation when it comes to hatching missionaries? Is the entire environment of the church conducive to breeding servants for the Lord? If not, what is missing and what must be changed? The aggressive local church has a central role in the road back.

Personal Sacrifice

If the war against the archenemy is to be won, if the downward spiral of candidates for lifetime service is to be halted, if the church is to move like a mighty army, some very basic and not-too-subtle changes must occur in our congregations.

Today church members lack for little of the finer things of life. Yes, some are wealthy, and that's not a crime. But most are average Americans. There are two cars in the garage, not because we are extravagant but because husband and wife go separate ways to their jobs. It's a fact of life, a necessity. In fact, Christian homes look pretty much like any other home. We have the same gadgets, the same brand names, the same TV special offers, and occasionally the same garage sales to try and unload some of this junk.

Most American Christians aren't extravagant. We are just part of the average American lifestyle. Our family rooms have the TV and the VCR. Our kitchens have the dishwasher and the microwave. Nothing fancy, just what every American household has.

But the lifestyle of America and our insatiable craving for everything that is new on the market is a serious hindrance to funding the missionary enterprise. Now don't get me wrong. American churches have given huge amounts of money to the missionary enterprise. But it's a drop in the bucket compared to what we spend on other things, things of little or no eternal value.

Unthinkable as it may be, perhaps American Christians should covenant with the Lord to do without some things the average American household has in order to fund an extraordinary adventure, an adventure against the very gates of hell. It is unlikely that we want to hear the proposals of the more radical Christian social reformers, those who say we ought to sell what we have and give to the poor (a Jesus suggestion) or that we should sell some of our property to help fund some of the overwhelming needs of the local church (a Barnabas action).

Oh yes, we are willing to pray. We are willing to give (within reason). We are even willing to sit through faded missionary slides at the annual missionary conference, but make a serious personal sacrifice so that those who have never heard the name of Jesus might hear and believe and be saved? That's asking too much. Personal sacrifice is out. Underwriting a year in the education of a young pastoral student can't hold a candle to that deluxe cruise we are planning.

But, thank God, some Christians have begun to see how insensitive we American Christians have become toward our financial responsibility in reaching the world for Christ. David Bryant points to a church in Arizona that pledged as much to world missions as the church did to its new $5,000,000 building program. That'll help get the job done. And 200 members of a California church sold their second cars while others mortgaged their homes in an effort to fund entirely a team of five couples to be missionaries to the Tonga tribe in Zambia. That'll help get the job done.[3]

These are genuine personal sacrifices, the kind most of us will never be willing to make. This year militant Muslim fundamentalists made greater sacrifices than these every day for their cause. The cultists made similar sacrifices every day for their cult. And the church of Jesus Christ in America? What did we do? We added a game room on the end of our house.

If the truth were known, and one day it will be, we American Christians could afford to do more, but we can't afford to do the same, and we dare not do less. The aggressive local church has a central role in the road back.

Church Giving

That things cost more today than they did a year ago is a fact of life. We have learned to live with it, even if we haven't learned to like it. Although the church has kept up with rising prices in insurance premiums, staff salaries and office supplies, some churches have not kept pace with missionary support. Others have done very well in making sure the missionary budget was tied to the church budget so there has been no slippage with regard to missionary support.

But everything we've done until now has not been enough. We continue to lose the battle. American churches have been the missions breadbasket for decades. Let's give credit where credit is due. As mentioned earlier, in 1988 American missions giving was a gigantic $8 billion[2].

That's a whopping amount, but look at it in context. Consider not what we have done, but what we could have done. In 1990, American evangelicals gave only 2.7 percent of their annual incomes to the Lord's work. And of the total amount given to church work, only a fraction of that went to world missions. The rest was used for maintaining the local ministry.

To add injury to insult, while the percentage of giving for American Christians lags behind the tithe guideline, the cost of missionary activity around the world continues to skyrocket. In 1980 the average monthly support for a missionary couple was $1554. In 1985 it was $2017. In 1990 it was $2581. Back in 1965 it was only $521. Every time we hear about the weakened dollar on the world market, we ought to bow our heads and pray for those missionaries in Japan, Germany, Switzerland, Israel, Brazil, or wherever inflation runs rampant and a dollar constantly buys less.

The aggressive local church has a central role in the road back. To win the battle will take more money. Surprised? Probably not. But churches and their memberships must come to terms with what that means. It means personal sacrifice. It means strengthening the ministry on the foreign field without weakening the home base. It means something else as well.

Planting Churches

"You can't ask me to do more! I'm giving all I can now! I have needs too!" Common complaints whispered under the breath at church stewardship banquets. While the churches of North America lag behind even a ten percent goal in giving, some Christians are already well beyond the tithe into sacrificial giving. They are struggling to help their church meet its present missions budget and are frustrated because their backs are to the wall and they can do no more. Can we ask them to do more just because enough isn't being done?

Maybe we don't have to. Maybe there's an acceptable, even desirable alternative that we have overlooked. That alternative is to distribute more evenly the responsibility.

We have already addressed the state of America's churches. They are not all large super churches as Sunday morning TV may lead you to believe. Most are small, probably smaller than the church you attend. And there are too few of them, large or small.

In America 96,000,000 people or 40 percent of the population are not affiliated with any religious group.[3] In addition to this, 100,000,000 people have little actual involvement with a local church. That in itself constitutes a vast mission field. Donald McGavran estimated that 1,500,000 new churches are needed in America.[4]

Beyond the need for new churches, many American churches are not healthy and, in fact, are in danger of demise. They can hardly be relied upon to be the breeding ground for world missionary activity.

Peter Wagner coined the term "church pathology" to describe those diseases which threaten the life of a church. In one large denomination usually thought to be strong, ten years ago Wagner calculated that up to 15,000 churches were in the process of dying.[5] The body produces cells to replace those which die constantly. Likewise, the body of Christ must plant thousands of new churches across America to replace those which are diseased or deceased.

There is an obvious and immediate result to planting churches in America. If the new church is built on new converts and not just disgruntled church hoppers, there will be a wave of evangelism sweep the USA as a wave of churches are planted. Men and women will trust Christ as Saviour. Homes will be put back together. Families will be strengthened. Moral and spiritual values will be changed. America will be better off.

But there is a subtle side effect to planting new churches in America. Fledgling assemblies will wish to follow the commands of Christ and early will be looking for missionary candidates to place on their church missionary budgets. The more churches we have, the more missions budgets we have. The more missions budgets we have, the more institutions training pastors and missionaries we can support; and the more pastors and missionaries trained, the more churches planted and missionaries sent around the world. It's a plan that can't fail, because it's a divine plan.

It becomes painfully evident that unless the church expands its home base, the whole foreign missionary enterprise will eventually collapse. Unless the local church gives greater emphasis to home missions, we can expect to see a gradual weakening in our foreign missionary outreach.

What can the local church do to halt the vanishing ministry and insure that funds are available to underwrite the missionary enterprise? Give more? That's one answer. Sacrifice more? That's another answer.

Sure, both of these answers are hard pills to swallow. A third answer is to recruit more men and women for lifetime ministry out of the ranks of the congregation, and a fourth answer is to plant more churches at home to broaden the base for missionary support and share the burden.

Manpower and money are the two necessities to get the job done. The ironic thing is that the local church holds the key to both of these. By the grace of God, we can get the job done, but it will take some serious shifts in the way we do things now.

The aggressive local church has a central role in the road back. The road back leads right down the center aisle of your church. No doubt it leads to your pew. And what is worse, it leads right through your sons and daughters and through your wallet. Who knows? It may lead right through you!

– 20 –

Sensitive Seasons

"To every thing there is a season and a time to every purpose under the heaven" (Eccles. 3:1).

If there is a season for everything, there must be seasons when a Christian is particularly sensitive to the movement of God upon his life. I call these sensitive seasons. They are important on the road back.

To be attuned to the movement of God in our lives is the practical goal of spiritual maturity. When we grow "in grace, and in the knowledge of our Lord and Saviour Jesus Christ" (2 Pet. 3:18), we more keenly see the footsteps and hear the heartbeat of God in our lives.

But even the most mature Christians would admit that there are certain times in our lives when the heartbeat of God beats more loudly in our ears. There are seasons in our lives when the footsteps of God make deeper impressions. These are our sensitive seasons, seasons in which we seem to be on the same frequency as God and our hearts are tender toward His will.

Sensitive seasons. Many of God's choice servants have experienced them. Take Jacob, for example. The life of Jacob is one of marked contrasts. He was saint and he was sinner. He took advantage of his brother Esau on every occasion he could. Jacob swindled Esau's birthright for what amounted to little more than a bowl of chili. Esau was understandably angry.

127

As Jacob fled from his brother, he made a stopover at a place called Luz, where he had a reassuring dream. Even though he had been wretched, God would bless him as He had Jacob's father and grandfather. Jacob awakened to exclaim, "Surely the LORD is in this place" (Gen. 28:16). A sensitive season.

Jacob's journey took him to the old country, the land from which his grandfather had journeyed. After a couple of decades he knew he must return home, even if it meant facing the wrath of his cheated brother. When he arrived back at the ford Jabbok, Jacob wrestled all night with an angel of the Lord. He boldly exclaimed to the heavenly grappler, "I will not let thee go, except thou bless me" (Gen. 32:26). Then and there his name was changed from Jacob (Supplanter) to Israel (Prince of God). The prince's first royal decree was to name the place Peniel (the face of God), "for I have seen God face to face, and my life is preserved" (Gen. 32:30). A sensitive season.

Years later the dreams of Joseph, Jacob's favorite son, caused jealousy to rage among the other brothers, and they conspired to kill the dreamer. Instead, they sold him into Egyptian bondage and told Jacob that his favorite son had been eaten alive by an evil beast. Jacob was anguished and mourned the supposed loss of Joseph many days. "And all his sons and all his daughters rose up to comfort him; but he refused to be comforted; and he said, For I will go down into the grave unto my son mourning" (Gen. 37:35). A sensitive season.

Yet Joseph was alive and once in Egypt was blessed by God and quickly rose to a position of power and prominence. When famine struck Jacob's land, he ordered his sons to go to Egypt to buy much needed grain lest they all starve. When the brothers came before the chief administrator of the Egyptian grain, they did not detect that it was their brother Joseph.

When Joseph revealed his identity to the brothers, after an astonishing moment of terrifying joy, they were sent back to the Promised Land to inform their father that Joseph was alive. "And they told him, saying, Joseph is yet alive, and he is governor over all the land of Egypt. And Jacob's heart fainted [but] when he saw the wagons which Joseph had sent to carry him, the spirit of Jacob their father revived" (Gen. 45:26-27). A sensitive season.

Sensitive seasons are not just emotional moments, but moments in which we bare our soul to God. Elijah had one when "the LORD passed by, and a great and strong wind rent the mountains, and brake in pieces the rocks" (1 Kings 19:11). But the Lord was not in the wind, nor in the earthquake that followed, nor the fire that followed that. Elijah's sensitive season came when the Lord spoke to him out of a "still small voice" (1 Kings 19:12). Elijah was in tune with God.

One of the men who was crucified with the Lord Jesus had a sensitive season as he hung on his cross next to our Saviour. When the other malefactor railed on the Lord, this man rebuked him, declaring that though they were justly punished, Jesus had done nothing amiss. Then, in a sensitive season, the man turned to Jesus and said, "Lord, remember me when thou comest into thy kingdom" (Luke 23:42).

Sensitive seasons, although they occur regularly, do not always bring spiritual success. Just as frequently, and perhaps much more frequently, these sensitive seasons end in rejection of God's still small voice.

The rich young ruler of Mark 10 is the only man recorded in Scripture to walk away from the Lord unhappy. His sensitive season began when he fell on his knees before Jesus and called Him "Good Master." When Jesus responded to his question about inheriting eternal life, the man "went away grieved" (Mark 10:17-22). He had a sensitive season. His soul was bared before God, but he rejected the movement of God in his life.

When Paul appeared before Felix, the Roman governor, and pressed him for a decision of faith, the Bible says, "Felix trembled, and answered, Go thy way for this time; when I have a convenient season, I will call for thee" (Acts 24:25). In waiting for a more convenient season Felix missed his sensitive season and died without Christ.

The same was true of King Agrippa. Paul faithfully ministered the Word to him and the king responded, "Paul, almost thou persuadest me to be a Christian" (Acts 26:28). But the sensitive season in Agrippa's life passed and so did the wooing of God.

Christians today have sensitive seasons just as these saints of old did. God is still the same, and He moves in our lives in the same way. The trouble is we frequently are not in tune with God. Our sensitive seasons come and go without ever being detected.

In these last years of the 20th century we need more than ever to be aware of sensitive seasons in our own life, and in the lives of others. The vanishing ministry is clearly related to an insensitivity toward these sensitive seasons. When God is moving in our life for ministry, we must do everything in our power to clear the clutter away, to silence the din of the world's clamor and to hear God's voice. And what we do for us we need to do for others.

If more and more Christians are to answer the call to lifetime service, more and more Christians will have to find themselves in situations where sensitive seasons are known to occur. Where are some of those places? What are some of the sensitive seasons of our lives? Please allow me to suggest a few.

Post Salvation Discipleship

When we are privileged to lead a person to the Lord or a person comes into the ranks of our church through salvation, there is a need for immediate discipleship. That person needs to be fed the milk of the Word and eventually God's meat. They need to be discipled.

The early period of discipleship is a sensitive season. This person has just passed from death unto life. He or she has just been born from above into the family of God. It is a sensitive season.

We owe it to our Lord to use this sensitive season to probe the possibility that God has saved our friend for a specific reason, and lifetime service to the Lord cannot be ruled out. The challenge to lifetime ministry should be an integral part of every discipleship program.

Spiritual Gift Seminars

Of the church's many needs today one of the greatest is for gifted, trained and dedicated workers. Perhaps the chief reason we do not have an abundance of such workers is that our people do not know what their spiritual gifts are.

After all, if we are saved to serve the Lord and the gifts given to us by the Spirit of God are the means by which we serve the Lord, and we do not know what our spiritual gifts are, how can we possibly hope to fulfill the purpose for which we are saved? It seems to me that the movement of the church is stymied when those who are to be perfected for the work of the ministry cannot be perfected due to lack of understanding and motivation.

When a church is engaged in faithfully identifying the spiritual gifts of its members, it is only natural for the members to encourage toward lifetime ministry those who obviously have the gifts necessary for such ministry. Hence, a spiritual gifts seminar in the local church in which every member is encouraged to attend, be instructed about the gifts and their use and to identify their own gifts and seek corroboration from other godly members, is the ideal sensitive season for God to move on a person's life for lifetime ministry.

Youth Missions Conferences

The annual church missions conference is usually a time of reporting. This is important and should be done. Missionaries need to be responsible to those from whom they receive support.

But is this the real goal of a missions conference? With the harvest fields so white and the laborers so scarce, should there not be another, overriding goal at a church missions conference?

Perhaps churches should consider a missions conference just for the teenagers of the church. If a missionary who has good rapport with young people was invited, one who has the burden of recruitment for the field, he would have a perfect opportunity to minister during one of life's most tender sensitive seasons — the teenage years.

Have you wondered, as I have, why our young people are bombarded every day with college recruiters, military corps recruiters, job recruiters and yet they are never approached by one of God's recruiters? Does it surprise you that the ministry is vanishing? It shouldn't! Youth missions conferences, specifically designed to recruit those tender to the leading of the Lord, are an idea whose time has come. It's a wise use of a sensitive season.

Camp Fireside Services

Today's Christian young people need something to commit themselves to. They need a cause, a flag to follow. Jesus Christ offers all of that and more, but many have stopped providing young people with the opportunity to commit themselves to Christ.

I am happy to say that there are still some Christian camps around where you can't leave from a week at camp without a commitment service. Usually it occurs on Friday night around a campfire. How many of us have committed or rededicated our life to the Lord at such a service? This is a prime sensitive season.

Christian camps must remain in tune with the movement of God in the lives of their campers. Unfortunately, during the last few years, many camps have just become recreational facilities. Oh yes, there is a speaker each morning and perhaps each night. But the talk of the camp, the reason to go, and the memories campers have after they've gone are all related to the pool, the three wheelers, the speed boats. There is little of that "spiritual talk" anymore.

Many camps have opted to receive hosts of inner city kids who have their way to camp paid by the State. This is a good evangelistic tool on some occasions, but the climate of the sensitive season is almost entirely removed. Discipline becomes a problem, and the atmosphere is all wrong for God's still small voice. Camps are an ideal setting for lifetime ministry recruitment, but they must continue to work at it.

Successes and Failures

If we are sensitive to the leading of the Lord, particularly good times for the movement of God come immediately after successes or failures.

College students who are unsure about the careers they are majoring in may well be in the midst of a sensitive season and not know it. Graduates who have majored in an area of interest to them and now find that the job market is closed to that interest may be experiencing a sensitive season.

Frequently students come to the institution I served to prepare for ministry after they had a business close or a farm fail. It was not that failure made them look toward ministry, but they became convinced that failure was God's way of moving them off center to follow the path to the center of His will.

Sometimes prime candidates for the moving of God in a life are those who have just experienced God's healing in their life. There is rarely a more sensitive season than when we think our life is over and God graciously grants us more years to serve Him.

Retirement

More and more, with the graying of America, students in schools of ministry are mid-lifers or retirees. It's not that they regret the years of their other career (although some do), it's just that God has given them good health and a strong desire to live out their days serving Him. After all, the Earl of Halsburg was 90 when he began preparing his 20-volume revision of English law. Galileo made his greatest discovery at age 73. Hudson Taylor was laboring vigorously on the mission field at age 69. Goethe wrote Faust at 82. And at age 85 Caleb wanted a mountain so that he could drive out a stronghold of giants (Joshua 14:10-15).

If these men can be active and productive at their ages, what can a retired IBM worker at age 55 do for the Lord? What can a retired or permanently furloughed auto worker do at a similar age? What can an Army career man at age 40 do for the Lord? What can a General

Electric engineer do after retiring at age 65? Ask Tom Allen.

Thomas Allen retired from General Electric at age 65 a few years ago and enrolled in Bible College to prepare for lifetime service to the Lord. His health was good, his mind was as sharp as a tack (he graduated magna cum laude) and his wife claimed hobnobbing with the younger students made him look and act years younger.

"To everything there is a season" (Eccles. 3:1). Sensitive seasons occur throughout our lives, but should we ignore the call of God, we have no guarantees that He will continue to deal with us during our sensitive seasons.

Every Christian who has read this far in this book can identify sensitive seasons in his or her life. Every Christian who has read this far can also identify whether or not they have listened to God's still small voice during those sensitive seasons. The road back will take honesty. What is God saying to you right now in this sensitive season?

– 21 –

Bridge Burning

It is likely that the road back will be covered with ashes. It will take a lot of men and women burning bridges behind them before we will see much progress in meeting the personnel needs of the pastorate or mission field.

Many who hear God's still small voice and vow to obey never make it to the field. In fact, some never make it to first base. What is the reason?

Fear! There is the fear of the unknown. There is the fear of stepping out and leaving all behind. There is the fear of selling homes and leaving friends to go to some distant place in preparation for lifetime ministry. Lacking the courage to take the first step is a severe deterrent to taking the second.

It is for this reason that when I meet a young couple who are convinced God wants them to go away to school to prepare for the ministry, I suggest they burn their bridges behind them immediately. The reason is simple. If you have burned your bridges, you can never go back. Jesus warned, "No man, having put his hand to the plough, and looking back, is fit for the kingdom of God" (Luke 9:62).

The call of Abraham is not unique, but it is interesting. God said to him, "Get thee out of thy country, and from thy kindred, and from thy father's home, unto a land that I will shew thee" (Gen. 12:1). There is no mention of destination, no promise of provision, no room for discussion. God had called Abraham, and in His time He would show the patriarch where and how he would live. Abraham's only concern was obedience. Bridges had to be burned.

There aren't a lot of Abrahams around today because we live in a society that has a penchant for future planning. We are up to our eyeballs in ten-year plans, most of which must be redone every year due to the mess of reality. Before we go, we must know where we are going, why we are going there, how long it will take to get there, what route will take us there, and most importantly, how soon we can come back if we don't like it.

Abraham was blessed of God because when he set out there were no guarantees, only God.

Many other men of God in the Bible have a similar story. Amos was a simple herdsman from Tekoa, not far from Jerusalem. God snatched him from the herds to be a spokesman for Him. There were no promises he would ever return to the pastoral life he loved so dearly. Bridges had to be burned.

Amos was blessed of God because when he set out there were no guarantees, only God.

And were the disciples of Jesus any different? Matthew 4 records that "Jesus, walking by the sea of Galilee, saw two brethren, Simon called Peter, and Andrew his brother, casting a net into the sea: for they were fishers. And he saith unto them, Follow me, and I will make you fishers of men. And they straightway left their nets, and followed him" (Matt. 4:18-20).

What an irresponsible act. Peter and Andrew were businessmen. They were fishermen. They had families, friends, perhaps financial obligations in the village. It would be totally irresponsible for them simply to leave their nets and follow the Stranger of Galilee. But they did. Bridges had to be burned.

Peter and Andrew were blessed of God because when they set out there were no guarantees, only God.

The next verses of Matthew 4 tell of James and John. "And going on from thence, he saw other two brethren, James the son of Zebedee, and John his brother, in a ship with Zebedee their father, mending their nets; and he called them. And they immediately left the ship and their father, and followed him" (Matt. 4:21-22).

Irresponsibility apparently ran rampant in those days in Galilean fishing villages. These two brothers heard the call of Jesus of Nazareth, and they immediately left not only their ship but their father in it. Who would see that the day's catch was marketed? Who would care for their father? How could these brothers be so thoughtless? But bridges had to be burned.

James and John were blessed of God because when they set out there were no guarantees, only God.

We have no reason to believe that the friends, families and financial obligations of these disciples were not well cared for. In fact, quite the opposite. But the point is that the call of Christ in our lives should be so overwhelming that no job, no craft, no house, no one can hold a candle to the One who loved us and gave Himself for us. When Jesus calls, we must burn bridges.

If God calls you to lifetime ministry, you can be certain that the first step will be the hardest. There will always be a host of reasons not to respond. There will always be reasons not to pack up and move to prepare for ministry. There is that low interest rate on your present house that you feel is foolish to give up. There is the fact that you could stay right where you are and support the work of the Lord done by others. There are always many reasons for not burning bridges and stepping out in faith, but there are never good ones.

When it was time for the children of Israel to cross the Jordan River into the Promised Land, they formed an impressive line of march. Everyone was anxious, but one group must have been apprehensive. They were the priests. Israel had been promised they would pass over on dry ground even though the Jordan was at flood stage. The priests were ordered to bear the ark of the covenant and march dead ahead toward the raging flood waters of the Jordan. I'm sure they didn't even like the expression "dead ahead."

But as soon as the feet of the priests touched the waters, they reared back and formed an unnatural pathway across the rocky bottom of the Jordan (Joshua 3:14-17). It was not until they got their feet wet, however, that they knew for sure they could trust God's promise to them. When they left their tents and started toward the Jordan, they had burned their bridges behind them.

The priests were blessed of God because when they set out there were no guarantees, only God.

When will we learn that with God we don't need other guarantees?

When will we learn that when God calls us to lifetime service, He wants all our yesterdays to be history? He wants all our bridges to be burned behind us.

Paul said, "Forgetting those things which are behind, and reaching forth unto those things which are before, I press toward the mark for the prize of the high calling of God in Christ Jesus" (Phil. 3:13-14). If the calling of God is so high, so heavenly oriented, why would we want to go back? Why would we not be eager to burn those bridges behind us?

If you are called to lifetime ministry today, claim the promise of Isaiah. "For the Lord God will help me; therefore shall I not be confounded: therefore have I set my face like a flint, and I know that I shall not be ashamed" (Isa. 50:7). It is possible to set your face like a flint only when you know the call of God is on your life. For when you know that, you know the blessing of God is on your life. There are no guarantees, only God.

When Jesus sent His disciples into the world of darkness, He said to them, "Fear not them which kill the body, but are not able to kill the soul: but rather fear him which is able to destroy both soul and body in hell. Are not two sparrows sold for a farthing? and one of them shall not fall on the ground without your Father. . . . Fear ye not therefore, ye are of more value than many sparrows" (Matt. 10:28-31). If He is interested enough to care for a little sparrow who stumbles and falls on the ground, don't you think He is interested in providing for you in lifetime ministry? You need to burn some bridges.

When Moses stood before the children of Israel he felt deep compassion for them. They would be going into the Promised Land and he would not. They would not have him to lead them and thus had a deep fear of the unknown, just like many who are called to ministry have before they take that first step to burn their bridges behind them. Moses didn't want to scare Israel, but he did want them to appreciate the obstacles they faced. So he told them straight out what to expect.

Deuteronomy 20:1 records his words. "When thou goest out to battle against thine enemies, and seest horses, and chariots, and a people more than thou, be not afraid of them: for the LORD thy God is with thee, which brought thee up out of the land of Egypt."

Every lifetime servant of the Lord should know that the enemy will always have more soldiers than we have. The enemy will always have more firepower than we have. The enemy will always have more money than we have. If we looked only at the enemy, we would never burn our bridges because we'd be crossing back over them in no time. But Moses didn't look at the enemy, and neither should we, for we have something the enemy doesn't have. We have the LORD our God.

With God before us and His angels beside us, there is no reason to have some old bridges behind us. The sooner you burn your bridges and take a step of faith toward your calling, the sooner you will realize that there are no guarantees, only God.

That's not a bad position to be in!

– 22 –

Spiritual Vision

The road back requires a new way of looking at things. The old way isn't bad, but it isn't good enough. If it were good enough, the ministry wouldn't be vanishing. We need spiritual vision.

Spiritual vision is that ability to see things as God sees them. That takes as much realignment of the heart as it takes focus of the eye. To see this world through God's eyes means we feel this world through His heart. For earthlings like us, that's easier said than done.

The road back will cause us to hearken back to things from the past, when more people appeared to be tender toward the leading of the Lord. One of the things I remember from my youth was the old principle of the three looks: the inward look, the outward look and the upward look. How does spiritual vision relate to these three looks?

The Inward Look

Looking inward is more than introspection. It is the application of the truths of God's Word to the life of His servant. When that happens, something wonderful occurs. We become spiritually attuned to God. We have the mind of Christ. We are filled with the Spirit.

As the lifetime servant of the Lord looks inward, he sees a glaring inadequacy — himself. Frankly, we are not equal to the task. If it were up to us, the vanishing ministry would continue to vanish, and the world would perish without Christ. Thank God it's not entirely up to us!

Paul cautions "every man that is among you, not to think of himself more highly than he ought to think" (Rom. 12:3). We need a good, hard look at ourselves, at our abilities and our inabilities. We dare not have an inflated opinion of what we have to offer the Lord.

Every useful lifetime servant has had some doubts about his own adequacy. Remember Moses? He's the guy who said, "Who am I, that I should go unto Pharaoh?" (Exod. 3:11). In essence God replied, "Moses, you're a nobody; just the kind of guy I need."

And what about Gideon? He was hiding from the Midianites at the winepress when he encountered God. Gideon protested to God, "Oh my Lord, wherewith shall I save Israel? behold, my family is poor in Manasseh, and I am the least in my father's house" (Judg. 6:15). Sounds like God's kind of man.

David's first appearance on the Sacred Page was not too auspicious either. Seven sons of Jesse were paraded by Samuel the priest; none were God's choice to be anointed as king. When asked if he had any more sons, Jesse replied, "There remaineth yet the youngest and behold, he keepeth the sheep" (1 Sam. 16:11). The whole tenor of Jesse's reply doesn't make David sound very promising as a potential king. Just the kind God was looking for!

Spiritual vision looks inward and doesn't see much in us, but it does see something exciting. No, we aren't much. But there is someone in us who is. To be a useful lifetime servant we must grasp more of the truth, "Greater is he that is in you than he that is in the world" (1 John 4:4). After all, it's "not by might, nor by power, but by my spirit, saith the Lord of hosts" (Zech. 4:6).

There is a truth taught again and again in Scripture that seems to escape the average foot soldier in the Lord's army. It is this. The battle isn't ours; it's His. We are just His infantry. This is His war.

What does the Bible say? "The Lord shall fight for you" (Exod. 14:14); "Let us flee from the face of Israel; for the Lord fighteth for them" (Exod. 14:25); "The Lord your God which goeth before you, he shall fight for you" (Deut. 1:30); "the Lord your God he shall fight for you" (Deut. 3:22); "For the Lord your God is he that goeth with you, to fight for you against your enemies, to save you" (Deut. 20:4).

The battle is the Lord's. Joshua believed this when he subdued the Promised Land. "For the LORD fought for Israel" (Joshua 10:14); "And all these kings and their land did Joshua take at one time, because the LORD God of Israel fought for Israel" (Joshua 10:42); "For the LORD your God is he that hath fought for you" (Joshua 23:3).

The battle is the Lord's. David believed this when he taunted Goliath saying, "And all this assembly shall know that the LORD saveth not with sword and spear: for the battle is the LORD's, and he will give you into our hands" (I Sam. 17:47).

The battle is the Lord's. The prophet Jahaziel believed this when a great multitude of Moabites and Ammonites came to battle against Jerusalem. He exclaimed, "Be not afraid nor dismayed by reason of this great multitude; for the battle is not yours, but God's" (2 Chron. 20:15).

A good, hard introspective look with spiritual vision will never find much of a soldier in us, but it will find one awesome Commander-in-Chief. The road back will demand that lifetime servants identify whose battle this is. Although we must admit our deficiency as soldiers and the dearth of new recruits volunteering for service, we must never admit defeat. The battle is the Lord's!

The Outward Look

Having looked into the interior of our being, the lifetime servant must look outward to the exterior circumstances of a world without God, without help, without hope.

The outward look starts with the world's phenomenal need. With 5.5 billion people in our world, and some 4 billion of them without Christ as Saviour, we cannot bury our heads in the sand. When 50,000 people die each day in our world, half of whom have never even heard of Christ, the urgency of doing something becomes apparent. When 37,000,000 Americans attend church on the average Sunday but 205,000,000 Americans do not, our outward look need not have telescopic vision. With 75 percent of America's teenagers unsaved and more unsaved people in the United States than in any other country in the world except China, Russia, India and Indonesia, we need to do some backyard outward looking.

But statistics will never move us to lifetime service; only compassion for the lost and a sense of God's call in our life will do that. Therefore, while we look outwardly, we must pray inwardly; pray that the Lord will not let us see statistics but people; pray that He will not let us see facts and figures but faces.

Jesus had an outward look when He was moved with compassion on the multitudes and said, "The harvest truly is plenteous, but the laborers are few; Pray ye therefore the Lord of the harvest, that he will send forth laborers into his harvest" (Matt. 9:37-38). This kind of perspective on the world takes more than a statistical analysis of the need. It takes a devastating vision of hell.

The finely clothed rich man died. His destination was certain, it was everlasting, it was excruciating. "And in hell he lift up his eyes, being in torments and he cried and said, Father Abraham, have mercy on me, and send Lazarus, that he may dip the tip of his finger in water, and cool my tongue; for I am tormented in this flame" (Luke 16:23-24). If the abode of the dead is this tormenting, the final agonizing torment of the damned in hell must be indescribable.

No mental image of hell will be graphic enough. The lifetime servant of the Lord must remember, however, that the only recorded person to experience life after death without Jesus Christ did all he could to get a message to his five brothers to keep them from the torment he would have to endure eternally.

Spiritual vision will require an outward look at the desperate world around us, but it also will require a look toward the outer darkness of hell before we will truly be stirred with compassion for the lost all around us.

The Upward Look

No Christian will be a useful servant of the Lord without an upward look toward Christ. After all, it is this look that brings salvation and convinces us that God is not willing that any should perish.

The upward look must be into the blessed face of Jesus. We must be like Peter, James and John at our Lord's transfiguration. "And when they had lifted up their eyes, they saw no man, save Jesus only" (Matt. 17:8). We must fasten our gaze on His gracious face, His nail-pierced hands, His nail-scarred feet.

But the one who is today our Saviour will one day be our judge. The upward look, therefore, also features a view of eternity. It drives us to do everything with the judgment seat of Christ in mind. We choose our careers with this in mind; we balance our checkbooks with this in mind; we raise our children with this in mind; we recruit the next generation of lifetime servants with this in mind.

The upward look makes us painfully aware that "we must all appear before the judgment seat of Christ; that every one may receive the things done in his body, according to that he hath done, whether it be good or bad" (2 Cor. 5:10). It's on this day that "every man's work shall be made manifest: for the day shall declare it, because it shall be revealed by fire; and the fire shall try every man's work of what sort it is" (1 Cor. 3:13).

Having spiritual vision means sifting everything we do to make sure our treasure is not on earth, "where moth and rust doth corrupt, and where thieves break through and steal" (Matt. 6:19). But the most acute focus of spiritual vision is the ability to look and clearly see where our treasure is, for that's where our heart is also.

A quick look at our calendar will tell us where our treasure is. A quick look at our checkbook will tell us where our treasure is. A quick look at our estate plan will tell us where our treasure is. And it will tell us a great deal about our heart as well.

The road back requires spiritual vision, in many cases spiritual tunnel vision. We must cut through all the hype about our personal esteem, cut through all the pathetic humor about partying with friends in hell and cut through all the values of this world, hell-bent for pleasure and promiscuity. We must see through all that to what is truly meaningful, eternally meaningful.

It's an old adage, but it's never lost its truth or its power: "Only one life 'twill soon be past; only what's done for Christ will last!" Everyone on the road back reflects on this adage often.

Conclusion

The mess of reality was not attained by a single person or group being diverted. We all were diverted. We all share the blame. And, thank God, we all have the opportunity to march in the Lord's army on the road back to victory.

Some of us must take a hard look at our children and have a heart-to-heart talk with them about lifetime ministry. This needs to start about the time they enter school. Dad and Mom, are you already a little behind as a heritage parent? Don't despair; playing catch-up is better than not playing at all.

Some of us must actively recruit young men and women around us for the greatest cause on the face of the earth. This, too, will mean a heart-to-heart chat and a place inked in on our calendars so that regularly we can disciple our budding Paul or Timothy.

Some will have to examine the road taken by the educational institutions we serve. We will want to ask whether the demands of the temporal have caused us to lose sight of the demands of the eternal. Are the graduates of the institution we serve less actively involved in eternal realities than they were a decade ago?

Some of us will have to rethink how much we need to maintain a standard of living commensurate with a dying world. Perhaps we will have to examine where our heart is, for there surely our treasure will be also.

More and more of us will have to say, "Here am I; send me," or the road back will lead us nowhere.

Although it is incredibly clear what we must do and why we must do it, what is not so clear is whether or not we will do what we must. It will take courage. It will take a new way of thinking, a new way of viewing ourselves and those around us. It will take spiritual vision. But most of all it will take decisive action.

When such decisive action was taken, David became the leader of Israel. When such decisive action was taken, Paul became the great apostle of the New Testament church. When such decisive action was taken, Luther began the Protestant Reformation. We don't need great men, for we have a great God. What we do need is decisive action.

Epilogue

A Call to Arms

Elijah was an unannounced prophet with an unwanted message. He was not perfect; no prophet was. He thought he alone had remained true to God when in reality 7,000 others had not bowed the knee to Baal. But Elijah was a man whose heart burned hot with a message from Jehovah.

At the height of Israel's idolatry under Ahab and Jezebel, the word of the LORD came to Elijah after a punishing drought of three and one-half years. God's people had to make a choice: would they continue to live with no consideration for God or would they begin to live in full submission to Jehovah? Elijah was chosen to focus their attention on that choice, and the contest with the prophets of Baal would provide opportunity for Israel to make their choice. Although they were God's people, they had been so assimilated into the culture of Baal that they could not clearly see their responsibilities toward God.

Gathered with wicked King Ahab and fearless Elijah on the top of Mount Carmel were 450 prophets of Baal and 400 prophets of the grove. In addition, all Israel stood in wonder at the contest about to begin.

I suppose the contest would never have taken place if the people had responded positively to Elijah's sentence sermon, but they did not. To the gathered throng the prophet bellowed, "How long halt ye between two opinions? If the LORD be God, follow him: but if Baal, then follow him" (1 Kings 18:21).

The people did not wish to respond, for their response would have been incriminating.

Although this same sentence sermon has been a valid question throughout the ages, it has never been more valid than in our day. "If the LORD be God, follow him: but if Baal, then follow him." The choice is still the same. Will God's people in the 20th century follow Christ or will they follow the god of this world? Will we sacrifice ourselves to eternal concerns or saturate ourselves in temporal pleasures? Will living the American dream keep us from bowing the knee to Jehovah?

Jesus reminds us, "No man can serve two masters: for either he will hate the one, and love the other; or else he will hold to the one, and despise the other. Ye cannot serve God and mammon [money]" (Matt. 6:24).

Does this mean that 20th-century Christians who chose the path of making money have fallen down before the pagan god Baal? Not necessarily so. Remember, God never said we could not have things. He only said things could not have us. "Seek ye first the kingdom of God, and his righteousness; and all these things shall be added unto you" (Matt. 6:33).

Some of the most godly people I know are also some of the wealthiest people I know. They have not bowed the knee to Baal. But many Christians have bowed the knee to the system of Baal, this world system. They have so imbibed the spirit of Wall Street, Madison Avenue, the Sunset Strip and Main Street America that they have become disoriented on the Calvary Road. They couldn't give up what they have now if they wanted to.

No, being wealthy isn't bowing the knee to Baal. Many poor people have bowed the knee to materialism and secular self-interest even though they have little to show for it. Bowing the knee to Baal is failing to submit our goals, our families, our finances, our lives and all that we have to the purposes and goals of Christ. It is settling down in the world and snuggling up to it so that the call of God in our lives is too faint to be heard.

Elijah called for a decision. "If the LORD be God, follow him: but if Baal, then follow him." What is the decision to follow God? Initially, it is a decision of the head. We must think it through. If we are to follow the Lord Jesus Christ as our Commander-in-Chief, is He someone worthy of our loyalty? Is He really God as He claimed to be? Did He really die for our sins? Did He really rise from the dead as He claimed? Is He worthy of our giving our life to Him in service? And, yes, if it comes to that, is He someone we would die for?

To follow Christ today is a decision of the head. We must get in our heads who He is and what He requires. We must get this in our heads so that the cultists, the Muslims, the religious quacks can't get it out of our heads. We must get it in our heads so that the university intellectuals can't shake our faith in Christ. We must get it in our heads so that the demons of hell cannot hamstring us. We must get it in our heads so that the pleasures of this world do not neutralize us.

To follow the Lord Jesus Christ rather than Baal and the self-fulfilling world system he represents is first a decision of the head. But more than this, if we are to follow Jesus as our Commander-in-Chief, it is also a decision of the heart. The power of the heart is infinitely greater than the power of the head.

With the head men understand; with the heart they believe. With the head men learn; with the heart they love. With the head men plan; with the heart they dream. Someone with a big head is thought to be a fool; someone with a big heart is thought to be a friend.

"And Jesus, walking by the sea of Galilee, saw two brethren, Simon called Peter, and Andrew his brother, casting a net into the sea: for they were fishers. And he saith unto them, Follow me, and I will make you fishers of men. And they straightway left their nets, and followed him" (Matt. 4:18-20).

The decision of Peter and Andrew to follow Jesus was not an intellectual one; it was a decision of the heart. Any who read *The Vanishing Ministry* and are moved by the Spirit of God to bring their lives into submission to the goals and purposes of God will do so, not as a decision of the head alone but also as a decision of the heart.

Head and heart are companions. They need each other like heat and light. When Elijah called for the people of God to stop hedging on serving God, he was calling for a decision of both the head and the heart.

But the decision to serve Jesus as Lord is more. It is a decision not only of the head and the heart but of the feet as well. There is a real sense in which following Jesus does not really get going until our feet get going.

"And as Jesus passed forth from thence, he saw a man, named Matthew, sitting at the receipt of custom: and he saith unto him, Follow me. And he arose, and followed him" (Matt. 9:9).

Matthew's head and heart believed that Jesus was the Messiah and Saviour of the world, but obedience began when his head and heart telegraphed a message to his feet. He arose and followed Jesus.

I don't for one minute believe the laborers are few today because God has somehow miscalculated how many laborers He needs to get the job done. I believe the laborers are few today because many of God's people who believe in their head that Jesus is God and feel in their heart that they should deny themselves and take up their cross and follow Him have never done either—denied themselves or followed the Master.

Much of the problem in the vanishing ministry is not with the head or the heart; it is with the feet. A head and heart following Jesus will no less affect our feet than a healthy flashlight battery will affect a flashlight.

Somewhere between "Yes, Christ is my Saviour, He is my Lord; I'll follow Him anywhere" and the fields white unto harvest something happens. Our feet become lame.

Perhaps we feel the fields have been closing anyway; there's no sense in our getting our feet going. But what about the 685,184,692 people of India, the 147,490,298 people of Indonesia, or the 147,404,375 people of Brazil? Those doors are not closed.

Or what about the 89,000,000 people of Mexico, the 55,800,000 people of the United Kingdom or the 55,400,000 people of France? Is the door closed to them? Not at all. The idea that the doors of the world are closed to the heart, to the head, to the feet of active Christians is absurd. It is the devil's diversion. Sure the field is closing, but it's not closed. Let's take our eyes off the closed world and focus on the billions of people who live in countries still open to the gospel. And then let's pray that the rest of the world will open again.

But when Elijah called for God's people to make a choice between the present comfort of living in Baal's world and the eternal reward of living in Jehovah's world, he knew that it was more than a decision of the head, the heart and the feet. He knew it was a decision of the life as well.

The same is true with you and me. Above all else, the call of Christ to "Follow Me" is a call of the whole life. If it weren't, it wouldn't be such a problem to us.

"Then said Jesus unto his disciples, If any man will come after me, let him deny himself, and take up his cross, and follow me" (Matt. 16:24). "If the LORD be God, follow him: but if Baal, then follow him" (1 Kings. 18:21).

Christ's call to every believer is to deny ourselves, to refuse our claims on our own life. It is a call to lose your life in His life, to lose your ideals in His ideals, to lose your goals in His goals, to lose your future in His future. If you would follow Christ, you must deny yourself.

Christ's call to every believer is also to take up the cross and follow Him. To lift high the cross of Christ above all else. To lift it high above personal preferences, high above family, friends, vocational goals. Hymn writer Elizabeth Clephane caught the spirit of this when she wrote, "I take, O cross, thy shadow for my abiding place; I ask no other sunshine than the sunshine of His face. Content to let the world go by, to know no gain nor loss, my sinful self my only shame, my glory all the cross."

This is a call to arms. High school students probably have never had a guidance counselor say to them, "Lift high the cross of Christ above your career opportunities." Empty-nesters who have seen the last of their children leave home have probably never had friends counsel them, "Lift high the cross of Christ above what you have worked for all these years." Retirees have probably never had their children say to them, "Lift high the cross of Christ above the ease of your golden years." But Jesus Christ says to you, "For whosoever will save his life shall lose it: and whosoever will lose his life for my sake shall find it" (Matt. 16:25).

How long halt ye between two opinions? The decision to follow Christ is a decision of the head, it is a decision of the heart, it is a decision of the feet, but it is also a decision of the life. How much whiter must the fields become before God's people make that decision? How much more depleted must the ranks of Christ's army become?

There has never been a better time to become a career soldier. The fields are white and getting whiter, and the laborers are few and getting fewer. Thousands of American pulpits are empty, and hundreds of thousands of towns of medium size and larger have no gospel witness at all. The average length of service in the 1980s on the foreign field was only between two and ten years, and the ranks of senior missionary leadership and field expertise grow dangerously thin.

There is a job to be done, and the church of Jesus Christ has the soldiers to do it, but too many of them want to be short-term volunteers or weekend warriors. Too many want to hold civilian positions at the base back home. Too few want to be front-line fighters.

Although we need civilians back at the base, we don't need as many as we have. The first command of God was to "be fruitful, and multiply, and replenish the earth, and subdue it" (Gen. 1:28), and every time a soldier chooses a career in business or medicine or education or technology we are obeying the command of God and subduing the earth, and that's good.

But the last command of Christ was, "Go ye into all the world, and preach the gospel to every creature" (Mark 16:15). Every time a soldier chooses to stay home and obey the first command of God, we reduce by one the ranks of those who can fulfill the last command of Christ, and that's an equation that cannot be eternally tolerated.

The vanishing ministry. Only you can do something about it!

Notes

Part One

1. David Bryant, *In the Gap* (Ventura, CA: Regal Books, 1984), p. 160.

2. W. Dayton Roberts and John A. Siewert, eds. *Mission Handbook*, 14th Edition, (Monrovia, CA: Missions Advanced Research and Communication Center, 1989), p. 53.

3. *Ibid.*, p. 53.

4. Bryant, *In the Gap*, p. 158.

5. Ralph Winter, "Countdown 2000!" *World Evangelization*, 15 (November December, 1988).

6. J. Herbert Kane, "A Brief History of North American Overseas Missions," in *Mission Handbook*, 10th Edition, Edward R. Dayton, ed. (Monrovia, CA: Missions Advanced Research and Communication Center, 1973), p. 9.

7. David B. Barrett and James W. Reapsome, *Seven Hundred Plans to Evangelize the World* (Birmingham, AL: New Hope, 1988) [5a].

8. Jim Reapsome, ed. *Pulse*, November 23, 1990, Vol. 25, No. 22 (Wheaton, IL: Evangelical Missions Information Service), p. 7.

9. Bryant, *In the Gap*, p. 160.

10. Elmer L. Towns, *The Complete Book of Church Growth* (Wheaton, IL: Tyndale House Publishers, Inc., 1985), p. 199.

11. C. Peter Wagner, *Your Spiritual Gifts Can Help Your Church Grow* (Ventura, CA: Regal Books, 1979), p. 199.

12. Bryant, *In the Gap*, p. 20.

13. David J. Hesselgrave, *Planting Churches Cross-culturally* (Grand Rapids, MI: Baker Book House, 1980), p. 77.

14. Donald A. McGavran, *Understanding Church Growth* (Grand Rapids, MI: William B. Eerdmans Publishing Company, 1970), p. 6.

15. Samuel Wilson and John Siewert, eds., *Mission Handbook*, 13th Edition, p. 59.

16. Reported by John Nordheimer (*New York Times*, October 24, 1983).

17. W. Dayton Roberts and John A. Siewert, eds., *Mission Handbook*, 14th Edition, p. 17.

18. Bryant, *In the Gap*, p. 158.

19. James F. Engel and Jerry D. Jones, *Baby Boomers and the Future of World Missions* (Orange, CA: Management Development Associates, 1989), p. 6.

20. Samuel Wilson and John Siewert, eds., *Mission Handbook*, 13th Edition, pp. 79-80.

21. W. Dayton Roberts and John A. Siewert, eds., *Mission Handbook*, 14th Edition, p. 10.

22. Samuel Wilson and John Siewert, eds., *Mission Handbook*, 13th Edition, p. 43.

23. Earl Parvin, *Missions USA* (Chicago: Moody Press, 1985), p. xi.

24. Donald A. McGavran, "Today's Task, Opportunity, and Imperative" in *Perspectives on the World Christian Movement*, Ralph D. Winter and Steven C. Hawthorne, eds., (Pasadena, CA: William Carey library, 1981), p. 549.

25. Ruth Siemens, "Secular Opinions for Missionary Work," in *Perspectives on the World Christian Movement*, Ralph D. Winter and Steven C. Hawthorne, eds. (Pasadena, CA: William Carey Library, 1981), p. 770.

26. Parvin, *Missions USA*, p. 10.

27. *Ibid.*, p. 10.

28. "America — The Mission Field," in *Focus on Missions*, (Cleveland, OH: Baptist Mid-Missions, February, 1987).

29. "America — The Mission Field," in *Focus on Missions*, February, 1987.

30. Parvin, *Missions USA*, p. 11.

31. "America — The Mission Field," in *Focus on Missions*, February, 1987.

32. George Gallup, Jr., *Religion in America* (Princeton, NJ: The Gallup Report, 1985), p. 40.

33. "America — The Mission Field," in *Focus on Missions*, February, 1987.

34. Parvin, *Missions USA*, p. xi.

35. W. Dayton Roberts and John A. Siewert, eds., *Mission Handbook*, 14th Edition, p. 52.

Part Two

1. *Campus Life*, February, 1987.

2. Lawrence A. Cremin, *American Education: The Colonial Experience 1608-1783* (New York: Harper and Row Publishers, 1970), p. 213.

3. John S. Brubacher and Willis Rudy, *Higher Education in Transition*, 3rd Edition. (New York: Harper and Row Publishers, 1976), p. 7.

4. Robert C. Pace, *Education and Evangelism: A Profile of Protestant Colleges* (New York: McGraw-Hill Book Company, 1972), p. 9.

5. Brubacher and Rudy, *Higher Education in Transition*, 3rd Edition, p. 10.

6. S. A. Witmer, *The Bible College Story: Education with Dimension* (Manhasset, NY: Channel Press, Inc., 1962), p. 30.

7. William Williams, *Personal Reminiscences of C. H. Spurgeon* (New York: Fleming H. Revell Company, 1895), p. 193.

8. *Ibid.* p. 193

Part Three

1. Stanley Lindguist, "Prediction of Success in Overseas Adjustment," in *Journal of Psychology and Christianity*, Vol. I, No. 2, Summer, 1982, p. 22.

Part Four

1. Mel Scarlett, *Preserving the Private College and Diversity* (Memphis, TN: A monograph published with the assistance of the Bureau of Educational Research and Services and the Department of Educational Administration and Supervision at Memphis State University, 1986), p. 9.

2. W. Dayton Roberts and John A. Siewert, eds. *Mission Handbook*, 14th Edition, p. 10.

3.   "America—The Forgotten Field," in *Focus on Missions*, February, 1987.

4.   Elmer L. Towns, *The Complete Book of Church Growth* (Wheaton, IL: Tyndale House Publishers, Inc., 1985), p. 104.

5.   C. Peter Wagner, *Your Church Can Be Healthy* (Nashville, TN: Abingdon Press, 1979), p. 28.

Appendix A

The State of Pastoral Training in America

In the fall of 1979, the American Association of Bible Colleges (AABC) contacted the Communications Department of the Wheaton Graduate School regarding the feasibility of a survey of Bible college graduates. The research was conducted by Kenneth Bosma and Michael O'Rear.

The Bosma and O'Rear study revealed some very heartening statistics for the Bible college movement. Most graduates appreciated their education, they had a clear vocational goal and were highly motivated to enter "full time Christian service."

But danger signs were evident as well. "The percentage of graduates who agree with the statement, 'When I enrolled in Bible college I had a clear idea of my vocational goal' is gradually decreasing: from 57% of the pre-1950 graduates to 44% of the 1970s graduates" (p. 69).

This decline prompted the need for additional and up-to-date information. The Kroll Survey came as a result of AABC's request for the author to present a paper at the American Association of Bible Colleges' annual meeting in St. Paul, Minnesota in 1986. That paper was entitled, *The State of Pastoral Training in America.*

In an attempt to provide the latest accounting of the health of pastoral training, the author prepared a questionnaire which was sent to American seminaries, graduate schools of religion, Christian liberal arts colleges, Bible colleges and Bible institutes. These institutions represented the spectrum of education, denomination and geography.

Included in this appendix are the following:

(1)   a sample of the questionnaire sent to the institutions
(2)   the results from responding Bible colleges listed by state and denomination
(3)   denominational totals for Bible colleges, Christian liberal arts colleges, Christian universities and Christian seminaries
(4)   movement within the pastoral major in responding Bible colleges
(5)   regional totals in responding Bible colleges

Significant among the results was the percentage of the total 1986 graduating class who were pastoral majors or declared their intent to enter the pastorate. In Christian seminaries the percentage was 48 percent; in Christian universities the percentage was 8 percent; in Bible colleges the percentage was 29 percent; and in Christian liberal arts colleges the percentage was 5 percent.

Reference: Kenneth Bosma and Michael O'Rear, *Educational Experiences and Career Patterns of Bible College Graduates* (Fayetteville, AR: American Association of Bible Colleges, 1981).

Pastoral Studies Questionnaire

The purpose of this questionnaire is to gather information from a variety of theological institutions to assess the state of pastoral training in America. Your time and effort in providing this information are appreciated.

INSTITUTION NAME _____

ADDRESS _____

YEAR OF FOUNDING _____ DENOMINATION _____

DEGREE PROGRAMS IN THEOLOGY _____

_____

● ●

What was the number of your graduates institution-wide in the Class of 1986? _____

What was the number of graduates with declared intent* to enter the pastoral ministry? _____

What number of your 1986 pastoral majors were female? _____

Which major in your institution had the largest number of graduates in the Class of 1986? _____

What was the number of graduates in this major? _____

Compared with other majors, has the percentage of graduates in your pastoral major over the last decade: (check one)

_____ increased _____ decreased _____ stayed the same

---

*Declared intent means the graduate intends to enter the pastoral ministry. Some institutions do not have a pastoral major per se, but have a general major in Bible or Theological Studies. Those students concentrating in pastoral studies in these majors have declared intent to enter the pastorate.

The Kroll Survey of Pastoral Training in America

Bible Colleges

Bible College State	Bible College Denomination	1986 Total Graduates	Total Pastoral Majors	Percent Pastoral Majors	Change	Largest Major
West Virginia	Independent	38	12	24	up	Pastoral
Pennsylvania	Baptist	152	24	16	up	Education
Massachusetts	Advent Christian*	26	10	38	up	Pastoral
California	Assembly of God**	103	33	38	same	Ministerial
Missouri	Interdenominational	86	23	27	same	Education
Missouri	Assembly of God**	176	135	76	same	Pastoral
Ohio	Christian Churches	103	42	41	up	Pastoral
Colorado	Christian Churches	75	38	51	up	Youth Min.
South Carolina	Interdenominational	136	45	15	same	General Min.
Iowa	Baptist	81	32	40	up	Pastoral
Indiana	Missionary Church*	72	18	25	same	Pastoral
Tennessee	Free Will Baptist	78	18	23	same	Pastoral
Nebraska	Independent	42	5	12	same	Missions
Tennessee	Christian Churches	71	22	31	same	Pastoral
Pennsylvania	Interdenominational	53	16	30	same	Pastoral
California	Four Square Gospel*	57	17	30	same	Pastoral
Oklahoma	Church of God	26	12	46	down	Ministry/Ed.
Illinois	Interdenominational	345	40	12	same	Bible/Theo.
Oregon	Interdenominational	209	31	15	up	Pastoral
Colorado	Church of Nazarene*	51	34	67	same	Pastoral
Minnesota	Assembly of God**	133	57	43	down	Pastoral
New Jersey	Interdenominational	33	7	21	down	Christian Ed
California	Churches of Christ	83	28	34	down	Pastoral
Pennsylvania	Interdenominational	82	23	28	same	Teacher Ed.
Michigan	Reformed Churches*	46	4	9	same	Missions
California	C & M.A.*	65	34	52	same	Biblical Lit.
Alabama	Interdenominational	30	10	33	same	Pastoral
Florida	Assembly of God**	151	46	30	same	Pastoral
Minnesota	C & M.A.*	108	23	21	up	Pastoral
Tennessee	Baptist	300	79	26	down	Education
Pennsylvania	Wesleyan Church*	52	22	42	same	Pastoral
Iowa	Interdenominational	26	11	65	up	Pastoral
Michigan	Interdenominational	31	3	10	down	Psychology

---

*   Listed as "Other" in the Bosma and O'Rear Study
**   Listed as "Pentecostal" in the Bosma and O'Rear Study
Interdenominational is listed as "Independent" in the Bosma and O'Rear Study

Pastoral Major Totals

Bible Colleges

Using the categories of Bosma and O'Rear in their 1980 study, the following totals were seen for various denominations within Bible colleges:

Denomination	1986 Total Graduates	Pastoral Majors	Percent Pastoral Majors
Baptist	611	153	25%
Christian	332	30	39%
Independent	1306	246	19%
Pentecostal	563	271	48%
Other*	503	174	35%

Of the colleges responding to the survey, the TOTAL NUMBER OF GRADUATES in the Class of 1986 was 3315. The total number of pastoral majors from these Bible colleges was 974. The percentage of Bible college graduates in 1986 who were pastoral majors was 29%.

---

* Those denominationally affiliated colleges which do not fall under the Baptist, Christian or Pentecostal categories.

Christian Liberal Arts Colleges

Denomination	1986 Total Graduates	Pastoral Majors	Percent Pastoral Majors
Baptist	482	20	4%
Independent	263	19	7%
Other	973	47	5%

Of the Christian liberal arts colleges responding to the survey, the TOTAL NUMBER OF GRADUATES in the Class of 1986 was 1718. The total number of pastoral majors from these Christian liberal arts colleges was 86. The percentage of Christian liberal arts graduates in 1986 who were pastoral majors was 5%.

Christian Universities

Denomination	1986 Total Graduates	Pastoral Majors	Percent Pastoral Majors
Baptist	781	69	9%
Independent	396	23	6%

Of the Christian universities responding to the survey, the TOTAL NUMBER OF GRADUATES in the Class of 1986 was 1177. The total number of pastoral majors from these Christian universities was 92. The percentage of Christian university graduates in 1986 who were pastoral majors was 8%.

Christian Seminaries

Denomination	1986 Total Graduates	Pastoral Majors	Percent Pastoral Majors
Baptist	93	76	82%
Independent	613	190	31%
Pentecostal*	49	31	63%
Other	747	430	58%

Of the Christian seminaries responding to the survey, the TOTAL NUMBER OF GRADUATES in the Class of 1986 was 1502. The total number of pastoral majors from these Christian seminaries was 727. The percentage of Christian seminary graduates in 1986 who are pastoral majors was 48%.

In comparison, then, the largest percentage of pastoral majors in the class of 1986 is to be found in the theological seminary (48%), followed by the Bible college (29%), the Christian university (8%), and the Christian liberal arts college (5%).

---

*   Only one responding institution

Bible College Majors Movement

With regard to increasing or decreasing numbers over the last decade in the pastoral majors at Bible colleges the following was learned:

Majors Movement	1986 Total Graduates	Percent Pastoral Majors	Pastoral Majors
Those indicating Pastoral Majors were increasing	1013	243	24%
Those indicating Pastoral Majors were constant	1639	518	32%
Those indicating Pastoral Majors were decreasing	606	186	31%

Little difference is discerned between institutions which have had the same or decreasing numbers of pastoral majors over the last decade. The institutions which have increasing numbers of pastoral majors are those institutions with the lowest percentage of pastoral majors currently.

Bible College Regional Percentages

Using the Bosma and O'Rear regional distinctions, Alaska/Hawaii (1), West Coast (2), Rocky Mountain (3), Southwest (4), Midwest (5), South (6), New York/New Jersey/Pennsylvania (7), and New England (8), how do pastoral majors fare in Bible colleges within a given region of the United States?

Region***	1986 Total Graduates	Percent Pastoral Majors	Pastoral Majors
1 (Alaska/Hawaii)	no Bible colleges represented		
2 (West Coast)	517	143	28%
3 (Rocky Mountain)	176	135	76%**
4 (Southwest)	26	12	46%*
5 (Midwest)	1099	270	25%
6 (South)	804	232	29%
7 (NY/NJ/PA)	372	92	25%
8 (New England)	26	10	38%*

With the exception of those regions where only one or two institutions were represented, the percentage of Bible college graduates in the Class of 1986 appears to be evenly divided throughout the regions of the United States.

---

*   Only one Bible college is represented in these figures.
** Only two Bible colleges are represented in these figures.
*** **Region 1:** Alaska, Hawaii; **Region 2:** California, Oregon, Washington; **Region 3:** Colorado, Idaho, Montana, Nevada, Utah, Wyoming; **Region 4:** Arizona, Oklahoma, New Mexico, Texas; **Region 5:** Illinois, Indiana, Iowa, Kansas, Michigan, Minnesota, Missouri, Nebraska, North Dakota, Ohio, South Dakota, Wisconson; **Region 6:** Alabama, Arkansas, Deleware, District of Columbia, Florida, Georgia, Kentucky, Louisana, Mississippi, Maryland, North Carolina, South Carolina, Tennessee, Virginia, West Virginia; **Region 7:** New Jersey, New York, Pennsylvania; **Region 8:** Connecticut, Maine, Massachusetts, New Hampshire, Rhode Island, Vermont